The
LORD *of the* FILMS

The LORD *of the* FILMS

THE UNOFFICIAL GUIDE TO
TOLKIEN'S MIDDLE-EARTH ON THE BIG SCREEN

J.W. BRAUN

ECW PRESS

Copyright © J.W. Braun, 2009

Published by ECW Press
2120 Queen Street East, Suite 200, Toronto, Ontario, Canada M4E 1E2
416-694-3348 / info@ecwpress.com

LIBRARY AND ARCHIVES CANADA CATALOGUING IN PUBLICATION

Braun, J. W.
The Lord of the films : the unofficial guide to Tolkien's
Middle-earth on the big screen / J.W. Braun.

ISBN-13: 978-1-55022-890-8 / ISBN-10: 1-55022-890-0

1. Lord of the rings, the fellowship of the ring (Motion picture).
2. Lord of the rings, the two towers (Motion picture).
3. Lord of the rings, the return of the king (Motion picture). I. Title.

PN1997.2.L67B73 2009   791.43'72   C2009-902532-9

Acquisitions editor: David Caron
Developing editor: Nikki Stafford
Cover and text design: Tania Craan
Front cover Hobbiton photo: Tanti Ruwani
Front cover Elvish illustration: Evan Munday
Typesetting: Gail Nina
Printing: Transcontinental   1   2   3   4   5

PRINTED AND BOUND IN CANADA

ECW PRESS
ecwpress.com

For Keely

Table of Contents

Foreword
By Clifford Broadway

Cliff Broadway, who played a Gondorian soldier in The Lord of the Rings *and hosted the Oscar parties where the cast, crew, and fans of the films celebrated their victories, is the co-author of* The People's Guide to J.R.R. Tolkien, *the cowriter/producer of the award-winning documentary* Ringers: Lord of the Fans *(2005), and (under the pseudonym "Quickbeam") a frequent contributor to TheOneRing.net, a popular website devoted to all things LOTR.*

For faithful readers and non-fans alike, the advent of Peter Jackson's *LOTR* film trilogy was a watershed moment in the history of popular culture. It was the surprise worth waiting over thirty years for. The success of the Trilogy was also a slap in the face to very ingrained Hollywood attitudes. Above all, it was a point of nexus between Tolkien's vast readership that had enjoyed his stories for years (typically embodied by the American counter-culture of the 1960s) and the newly-sprung kids who had MTV attention spans and expectations of instant CGI gratification from their movies.

Who could have ever figured these two camps would join so easily under one tent of fandom? Who could foresee in their watery Elven mirror such disparate audiences coming together and melding en masse? Not me. And I was smack in the middle of it all when it happened, yet still I had to pinch myself. No one could have predicted the marriage of old-school Ringers and those novice younglings so eager for hobbity goodness. It was a synthesis of different people who did not always want the same thing from Peter Jackson. To be sure, the first group wanted — demanded — fidelity to the source. The second group was feeling so let down by George Lucas they just wanted to be entertained by a ripping good story. New Line Cinema just wanted to get their money back.

There are few comparisons that fit what happened between 1999 and 2004 — the time between the first rumors of an *LOTR* film production moving forward, and the ultimate conclusion where *The Return of the King* smashed all those Oscar records with a clean sweep at the Academy Awards. There is nothing else in movie history to match this amazing thing.

A certain alchemy happened. Despite the counter-intuitive obstacles set against the project, despite Jackson being untested against such demands, it all came together in a wave of magic, confluence, and grand-scale luck. The intrepid Kiwi director showed considerable pluck in even approaching the whole damn thing. I would have given him credit just for trying it out. That he achieved mind-blowing financial and critical success, and satisfied the deepest desires of incongruent fans, is a testament to his skill. It makes me wonder sometimes.

In Jackson's hands we see how *The Lord of the Rings*, such a sprawling and difficult book, was made imminently digestible to the popular taste of *fin de siècle* audiences. I think that's the true key to his success: he made it all go down easy. Don't you think he made quite a fun ride out of it?

Now along comes J.W. Braun — as clever a Ringer as you could hope to meet — with his new book *The Lord of the Films*. Here the same magic of synthesis and mass-appeal is at play. Here is another proof of how much fun we can have paring down a behemoth to the glorious nitty-gritty.

This is an almanac of all things relevant to the film adaptations, liberally sprinkled with gentle humor. It was not an enviable task. I can't imagine the chore of combing through so many theatrical screenings, so much DVD content, so many fan events and slogging interviews, just to bring this stuff down to one wee volume. J.W. has taken a very large filmic experience and (here comes the foodie metaphor) reduced it down to a fine glaze. His knack for chasing down ephemera is marvelous. It's a book overflowing with juicy bits. Here we can take it all in (once more) and gain a new perspective on the cinematic incarnations of Tolkien's world.

As I said, making it all go down easy is the real trick. And J.W. did exactly that.

Having this wealth of information handy while I re-watch Jackson's films — especially with friends who are experiencing *LOTR* for the first time — makes it all so much better. *The Lord of the Films* goes a long way toward giving newbies the best trivia injection ever.

Peter Jackson's epic film trilogy stands on its own — to be adored and rewatched throughout our lifetimes. These are the films you share with your kids, explaining to them as you watch the intricate paths of who, what, and why; and further engaging their young minds in the greatest narrative of Life that the Professor could have given us.

And now we have the ideal guidebook to take along for the ride.

Cliff Broadway (Quickbeam)
Los Angeles
April 2009

Introduction
About This Book

"You do realize your performance as Gandalf will outlive us all, with each new generation discovering the magic of these films, right?"

Back in 2000, when Ian McKellen had his email address posted online for the world to see, and any crazed fan of the upcoming *Lord of the Rings* films could send him hyperbole, he received the above email. In this case, however, while the fan (which was me) probably *was* crazy, the words were more than mere hyperbole. The films have already enchanted folk from all around the world and are recognized as fantastic cinematic adventures filled with good and evil, swords and sorcery, epic battles, and true romance.

This book serves as your guide to Middle-earth on the big screen. Through its pages, you'll discover the true magic of the incredible live-action *Lord of the Rings* films. This guide can be read two ways. Reading it cover to cover like a conventional book will allow you to learn about the journey of these films, giving you the story of their creation from beginning to end. You might also enjoy reading this book while simultaneously watching the films, allowing you to watch them with a new appreciation or to look for details you missed before.

This book is *not* a substitute for watching the films or reading the books they are based on. It would be pointless for me to retell a story that has already been told so well on the page and on film. What I will do, however, is go beyond the films to provide a deeper understanding. This means, of course, that out of necessity this book contains *Lord of the Rings* plot spoilers. If you've not yet seen the films, I urge you to watch each of them at least once before using this guide. *The Lord of the Rings* books are magnificent too, and well worth reading; however, no knowledge of the books is necessary to understand or enjoy this book.

You might know that there are two different versions of each film.

However, if you've only seen one version, don't panic! Most of the information in this book applies to whatever you've seen. Occasionally, however, I'll specify one version. The "short" versions, released theatrically before being released on DVD, are referred to as the "theatrical cuts." The longer versions, released on DVD some months later, are referred to as "extended editions."

As we go scene by scene through *The Lord of the Rings*, you'll see that each section has a title followed by a brief summary of whatever part of the film it covers. You'll then find four subsections. For fun, they are named after the Free Peoples of Middle-earth:

What the Big Folk Were Saying
"The big folk" is what Hobbits call people like you and me. These are comments from ordinary folk that were overheard in the movie theaters.

What the Wizards Know
Here you'll find behind the scenes information I gathered from numerous sources over the years, giving you the inside scoop on the development of the films.

What the Elvish Eyes and Ears Have Noticed
These are little details in each scene you might not have noticed and can look for the next time you watch the films.

The Foolishness of a Took
These are mostly bloopers, production errors, or nitpicks.

Along the way, you'll also see sidebars with compilations of information. Some help tell the story of how these films were made, but others are simply for fun.

I've also included "Easter Egg Alerts," which apply only to the Platinum Series Special Extended Editions (the four disc sets). Easter eggs are hidden bonus features that don't appear in the DVD menu. While none are included in the other sets, there are several in the original extended edition releases.

Please keep in mind that a dozen people watching the same film will have twelve different experiences, and this book can't contain every opinion. But in addition to my own observations, I've included interviews I conducted with some of the people who worked on *The Lord of the Rings*. These designers, artists, and actors share with us the experience of working on the films, and tell us what they think about the trilogy. Of course, the opinions shared in this book are not meant to supersede the reader's thoughts and experiences, but only enhance them with more information and ideas.

Finally, knowing that *Lord of the Rings* fans are some of the most intelligent, active people out there (in my completely unbiased opinion), I threw in some games at the end of the book to challenge you.

So prepare to rediscover the haunting beauty, mysterious sorcery, and powerful forces of Middle-earth as we journey together. Prepare for *The Lord of the Films*!

From Book to Film
A One Ring Circus

Unless you've been living in Gollum's cave, you're probably aware that before *The Lord of the Rings* was a trilogy of films, it was a set of books.

J.R.R. Tolkien became a popular author quite by accident when *The Hobbit*, a story he had written for his children, came by chance to the publishing firm George Allen & Unwin. It was published in 1937 and became an instant classic, leading fans (and the publisher) to ask for a sequel. After many years of hard work (and procrastination), Tolkien finished *The Lord of the Rings*, and it was published in three volumes in 1954 and 1955.

By the time of Tolkien's death in 1973, the books had become popular enough to capture the attention of the film industry. Hollywood didn't understand the books, of course, but saw dollar signs in the property, and various studios looked into the possibility of a film adaptation. Ralph Bakshi, a director and Tolkien fan, thought three animated films were the way to go, and he successfully got the rights into the hands of producer Saul Zaentz, with whom he had worked before. However, a trilogy was an ambitious idea, and Bakshi was quickly asked to make it two films. Despite deadline pressure, Bakshi delivered Part One on time, but that's about all that went well. The distributor, United Artists, figured more people would want to see the whole *Lord of the Rings* than half of it, so they dropped "Part One" out of the title and marketed the film as if it were the complete story. In 1978 it hit the theaters, and the duped audiences made Denethor look like a happy guy by comparison. Meanwhile, Zaentz decided not to go through with Part Two, forcing Bakshi to spend the next three decades answering questions about why he didn't finish what he started.

However, as one director's quest ended, another began. During the film's run at the Old Plaza Theatre in Wellington, New Zealand, a curly-haired seventeen-year-old was introduced to Middle-earth, and

Ralph Bakshi (left) and Saul Zaentz (right) worked together to make an animated adaptation of The Lord of the Rings. (Victoria Bakshi Yudis)

shortly afterward the young man bought a copy of *The Lord of the Rings* featuring the film's tie-in cover art. His name was Peter Jackson, and a couple decades later he would become an established writer and director in the film industry while simultaneously witnessing a change in the business. Back when Bakshi made his film — and throughout the '80s — if films needed special or visual effects they had to use an expensive, experienced company, or the effects would look silly next to *Star Wars* and the other big budget films. (You can see why Bakshi, who didn't have a lot of money to spend, bypassed the problem by using animation.) Furthermore, the effects were limited by both physics and the ingenuity of these contracted workers, and writers were forced to consider this when writing scripts. However, in the early 1990s, Jackson saw that digital technology was about to change this. Effects were moving into a new realm, that of hardware and software. In 1993, Jackson bought a computer, cofounded his own effects house, Weta Digital, and began preparing scripts with his own company in mind.

Two years later, Weta had thirty computers, and Jackson and his partner Fran Walsh, who were working on *The Frighteners* (1996), began to wonder what an ambitious project for Weta could be. They thought about a fantasy film, agreeing that the story had to have depth. "Like *The Lord of the Rings*." It needed a sense of reality. "Like *The Lord of the Rings*." And yet have an element of magic. "Like the . . . Hang on, could we do *The Lord of the Rings*?" They assumed the rights were sure to be tied up or unavailable, but made an inquiry nonetheless.

At the time, Jackson and Walsh had a "first look" deal with Miramax; practically anything they wanted to do had to be offered to this studio first. By coincidence or fate, Miramax was busy at that time with *The English Patient* (1996), produced by a guy named Saul Zaentz — who still controlled all rights for *The Lord of the Rings*. Jackson talked to Miramax, Miramax talked to Zaentz, and Zaentz, of course, said . . . "not interested" to Jackson's and Walsh's idea.

Right now, you're probably saying something along the lines of Fred Savage's character in *The Princess Bride*: "You're reading the story wrong!"

In fact, Zaentz had said no to many people who had made inquiries over the years. The producer did not want to be burned again. This was a guy who was used to winning the Oscar for Best Picture, and he once said the only production of his he wasn't satisfied with was that darn animated *Lord of the Rings*.

It would have been the end for Jackson's and Walsh's idea, but they had Miramax interested, and this studio had a trump card to play. You see, *The English Patient* was supposed to be financed by 20th Century Fox, but just as filming was to begin that studio backed out. It was Miramax that stepped in and saved the day. The film went on to win nine Oscars, and Zaentz knew he owed Miramax big-time. After nine months of negotiations, Miramax acquired the rights to make *The Lord of the Rings*, and in 1997 preproduction began on the greatest film adventure in history.

Jackson and Walsh wanted to begin with *The Hobbit* and (assuming that was a success) move on to the *Lord of the Rings*. But Zaentz didn't own all the rights to *The Hobbit*, so Miramax decided to skip it and get right into *The Lord of the Rings*. With no successful prequel, the studio wasn't willing to finance three films right out of the gate; it gave the green light for two. (This sounds familiar, doesn't it?) Not that Miramax's owner, the Walt Disney Company, looked at then as

Peter Jackson has been described as cool as an elf, mad as a wizard, and cuddly as a hobbit. (Ian Smith)

two. To Disney's chief executive officer, Michael Eisner, Miramax was making one film, and he wouldn't allow the studio to spend more than $75 million on it.

In the past, $75 million had been a lot of money. (And to most of us it still is.) But as previously mentioned, the film industry was changing, and by the late 1990s nine figures was no longer a monster budget. Indeed, films such as *Titanic* (1997) and *Star Wars: The Phantom Menace* (1999) made $100 million budgets look downright modest. As the *Rings* project progressed, $75 million began to look woefully inadequate for two films heavily dependent on special effects.

Miramax, under pressure from Disney, had no choice but to ask Jackson to make one two-hour film. When he refused, the project threatened to unravel for everybody. Jackson's agent, Ken Kamins, knew Miramax was going to bring in a new writer and director; so he came up with a proposal he hoped would please all sides. He asked that Jackson be allowed to find another studio willing to finance two films as well as pay Miramax the millions already spent. Ready to pull out, Miramax agreed to these terms and gave Jackson four weeks to find a new backer.

In the ten years preceding this, New Line Cinema had earned a reputation as a maverick studio, making experimental films that were slightly different from the mainstream. Sometimes this was profitable; *Dumb and Dumber* (1994), *The Mask* (1994), and *Austin Powers* (1997) struck a chord with filmgoers and made millions. Sometimes this was less so; repeated attempts to make Hulk Hogan a movie star never worked. The bigger problem for New Line was that when it made a blockbuster, the stars often wanted much more money to reunite for a sequel. Hence, audiences were given new casts for *Dumb and Dumberer* (2003) and *Son of the Mask* (2005). Sequels, with their built-in audiences and bankable opening weekends, are the lifeblood of the film industry, and New Line Cinema was looking for a solution to the problem. What the studio really needed was a property that already had a devoted audience, with a chance to film the sequels before the actors became big stars.

New Line executive Mark Ordesky, a *Lord of the Rings* fan who had worked with Jackson previously, arranged for Jackson to give New Line a presentation. But it was Ordesky's boss, Bob Shaye, who ultimately decided the films' fate. When the presentation came to a close, Shaye looked at Jackson and said, "I don't get it. Why would you want to charge nine dollars to see this when you could charge twenty-seven?"

A confused Jackson needed a moment to work out what Shaye was talking about. "You think there should be three movies?" Jackson asked.

On that July day in 1998, the films as we know them were born.

Q&A
with Artist Paul Lasaine

As production illustrator, visual effects art director, and scenic unit director, Paul Lasaine came up with the look and feel for many of the places of Middle-earth, and helped integrate the art with the live-action footage. On May 27, 2005, just after the films had all been released on DVD, he answered some questions for me.

Braun: How did *The Lord of the Rings* enter your life?

Lasaine: *The Lord of the Rings* really entered my life when I got the call to work on the films. I had never read the books, though I had read *The Hobbit* twice, years ago, and had tried to read *The Lord of the Rings*, but had never got past the party. Little did I know what I was missing! I think J.R.R. made that first part difficult to get through on purpose, to weed out the riffraff. When I got the call to work on the film I was happily employed at DreamWorks Animation. I was an art director there, and I'd been at DreamWorks for about four years. Before that, I had been the head of Matte Painting at Disney Studios' Visual Effects division called Buena Vista Visual Effects.

It was June 1999 when Barrie Osborne, the *Lord of the Rings* producer, called me out of the blue from New Zealand. At first my impulse was to turn him down. After all, I was under contract with DreamWorks. I had a house, a wife, and a dog. Putting life on hold, packing up, and moving to New Zealand wasn't really in my plan at the moment. My wife Tina simply said, "We're going! Right?!"

Three weeks later I was on a plane bound for New Zealand.

Braun: Did they know of your ignorance?

Lasaine: On the phone with Barrie, I told him I had never read the books. He said it wasn't a problem; they already had their "Tolkien experts" (John Howe and Alan Lee) working on the designs. What they needed was someone with experience as a film designer who could take Alan's and John's designs and make them cinematic.

I started reading the books on the plane to New Zealand. This time I got past the party! When I got to the part where we're introduced to the Nazgûl for the first time, I began to understand what all the hoopla was about. I was hooked.

Two weeks after my wife and I hosted a Fourth of July party at our house, I arrived in New Zealand. It was July 18, 1999. Summer, right? Wrong! Welcome to Wellington. I think they have the worst weather I've ever experienced (sorry to all my Kiwi mates — it's true)! All the travel brochures of New Zealand that I looked at showed an almost tropical paradise, complete with beaches.

When I got off the plane, I knew I'd packed wrong. I would soon come to fall in love with Wellington, but as I was driven from the airport to my apartment (on the "wrong" side of the street, by the way) in near hurricane winds, complete with horizontal rain, all I could think was, "What the hell am I doing?"

The next day when I reported for duty at Stone Street Studios, a converted paint factory just off the runway of the Wellington International Airport, the weather was worse than the day before. I was disoriented and jet-lagged. Five things happened that day:

- I met Alan Lee, who would be my office mate for the next six months.
- I wandered around the Art Department and dug through all the design drawings Alan and John had done over the past two years.
- I read the script for *The Fellowship of the Ring*.
- I met Peter, who gave me a personal tour of the studio and Weta.
- I learned how to use the espresso machine in the studio kitchen.

It was there, toward the end of that first day, staring out the window at the storm, rain pelting the glass, a 747 thundering down the runway, drinking the best latte I'd ever had, that I realized we were going to win a boatload of Oscars.

Looking back on that day, I think most of us knew that we were working on something special. Of course we were all pleased by the box office returns, and the Oscar count, but that all pales in comparison to just how cool it was to actually work on a project that we all knew was going to make such a huge impact on the film world.

Braun: Did you ever finish the books?

Lasaine: It took me an entire year to finish the books. Normally I would have read them faster, but I was pretty busy on the show, and I wanted to devour every word. I would read every night before I went to sleep, but that was pretty much all I had time for. Plus, I wasn't reading them for pleasure; I was studying them — using them as "text books" to Middle-earth. When I started work on a specific location, however, I would be sure to read those pages that pertained to it.

Not having finished the books only got me into trouble once: one of my first illustrations, a painting of Lothlórien, had the Fellowship ascending a Mallorn tree. I hadn't quite gotten to that part in the books yet, so I dutifully read the section that described the Golden Wood and the Mighty Mallorn trees. How was I to know that

Gandalf (theoretically) dies before the Fellowship reaches Lothlórien? So of course, I included him in the group. Somehow the painting ended up in the first internet trailer, and the shock waves followed. Peter had a bit of a chuckle over the whole thing, and was actually happy to throw everyone "off the scent."

Braun: If Jackson makes *The Hobbit* into a film someday, how do you think it should be done?

Lasaine: Well, obviously it should have the same flavor as *The Lord of the Rings*, but I'd like to see it be a lot less dark — more fun and adventurous . . . like the book. If Peter does it, he'd have to keep the "zombie" thing to a minimum. Ian McKellen should certainly be in it as Gandalf. It could be interesting to see Elijah Wood play a young Bilbo. Beyond that, who knows.

Braun: What do you think of *The Lord of the Rings* film trilogy as a whole?

Lasaine: All in all, I'm extremely pleased. Sure, there are a couple things I would change — a cut here, an effect there — but on the whole, the results surpassed even my expectations of that first day. Actually, in many ways, it's hard to be objective. I was talking to my wife about this just yesterday. We lived in New Zealand for almost two years, and *The Lord of the Rings* became so much a part of our lives, that watching it isn't like watching a movie at all. It's more like flipping through the pages of a scrapbook. Every scene has a memory for us.

The Fellowship of the Ring

(2001)

(Jacquie Roland)

Directed by: Peter Jackson

Starring:

Elijah Wood as Frodo

Ian McKellen as Gandalf

Viggo Mortensen as Aragorn

Cate Blanchett as Galadriel

Hugo Weaving as Elrond

Theatrical Cut: 2 hours 58 minutes

Liv Tyler as Arwen

Rated PG-13

Orlando Bloom as Legolas

Released December 19, 2001

Ian Holm as Bilbo

Sean Bean as Boromir

Extended Cut: 3 hours 28 minutes

John Rhys-Davies as Gimli

Rated PG-13

Christopher Lee as Saruman

Released November 12, 2002

Sean Astin as Sam

Billy Boyd as Pippin

Domestic Gross: $314,776,170

Dominic Monaghan as Merry

Worldwide Gross: $871,368,364

Sala Baker as Sauron

The Fellowship of the Ring follows the story of the One Ring from its creation to the breaking of the Fellowship formed to protect it. It's an episodic road movie, taking us from Hobbiton through Bree, Rivendell, Moria, and Lothlórien before climaxing with the battle at Amon Hen.

You already know this is one of the great films of our lifetime, a keepsake we will always treasure. Why is this so? Because *The Fellowship of the Ring* puts formula blockbusters to shame by breaking all the rules, making up new ones, and making them work.

Unlike most previous book adaptations, this film is not a companion for the book it is based upon, neither requiring its knowledge, nor enhancing the experience of reading it. You might as well forget everything you've read in Tolkien's *Lord of the Rings* for the film's duration, as Jackson's adaptation feels free to change not only what the characters say, what they look like, and how they act, but their knowledge and motivations. The filmmakers did not try to make a great interpretation of the book, they tried to make a great film. They succeeded. *The Fellowship of the Ring* ultimately redefined the gold standard for fantasy films and book adaptations.

Not that I believe it is a perfect film, either in theatrical or extended form. In the former, the action sequences outweigh the quieter moments, and there isn't a lot of character development. In the latter, the momentum is sluggish, and there's not much of a rhythm established. However, both versions feel perfect at times. The music, the acting, the direction, and the cinematography are as good as can be, and often they are all working in concert with each other, leading to "wow" moments.

The film might even improve upon its source material in some ways, creating greater character arcs for Aragorn and Boromir, and giving the hobbits a more proactive role in the Fellowship.

Can we now discard the book? No. A great number of characters, many details, and most of Tolkien's brilliance remain only in the text. Will the film live on, entertaining old and new fans with each successive generation? Without a doubt. It's a magical journey every person should take sometime in his or her life.

Prologue

The history of the Ring is recounted, from its part in an historical battle to its rediscovery by Bilbo.

Power can be held in the smallest of things. (J.W. Braun)

What the Big Folk Were Saying

"Hey, you skipped page 33!"
　　— Someone shortly after the film begins

"It's a kitchen appliance gone bad!"
　　— A man referring to Sauron

What the Wizards Know

Back in the 1980s, when Jackson was a young man shooting his own movies as a hobby, he had to mail his 16 millimeter film to a laboratory for development along with a form that asked for (among other things) his production company's name. Rather than leave this space blank, Jackson listed "WingNut Films" as a joke. Wingnut was a pet rabbit (with floppy ears that looked like the hardware he was named for) that briefly lived at the headquarters of the *Evening Post*, the New Zealand newspaper Jackson worked for at the time. The rabbit has since died, but his name lives on.

The Lord of the Rings title was the last shot to be finished for this film.

When Peter Beagle, author of *The Last Unicorn*, rewrote Chris Conkling's script for the 1978 animated adaptation of *The Lord of the Rings*, he created a new beginning to the story: a prologue covering the history of the Rings. It seems another Peter agreed that was a good idea.

The prologue for *The Fellowship of the Ring* was originally conceived as being narrated by Frodo. Then, Gandalf was deemed a better choice. Finally, Galadriel was chosen to give the voiceover, because her character and Blanchett's voice seemed perfect for the part.

Tolkien thought up the "One Ring to rule them all" verse while in the bathtub.

Jasmine Watson, just a few years out of school, designed most of the jewelry for the films. She has said her favorite piece is Nenya, Galadriel's Ring of Water.

The One Ring was designed and created by Jens Hansen just prior to his death in 1999.

Weta Workshop, the trilogy's physical effects company, had a number of problems designing weapons and armor until they got some unexpected help. John Howe, brought onboard as a conceptual artist, happened to be an expert in medieval design. (He even brought his armor and weapons with him to New Zealand.) With his aid, Weta produced designs that were both realistic and beautiful.

Playing the titular character of a multibillion dollar film trilogy is an impressive addition to an actor's resume. Here, the honor does not go to a star such as Elijah Wood, nor to a legend such as Christopher Lee, but to stuntman Sala Baker, who appears for one minute and thirty-two seconds as Sauron, the Lord of the Rings.

Hobbits, and Wizards, and Dwarfs (Oh My!)
A Book of Lost Scales

Tolkien could give us Hobbits, Dwarves, Elves, Wizards, and Men without having to worry about scale issues. The films were not so lucky. Had the filmmakers decided to cast parts with size in mind, the pool of possible actors would have been limited, and we might not have seen the perfect Bilbo, Frodo, or Gimli. Computer generated images had not advanced far enough to handle four hobbit heroes for three films. This led to the decision to cast average sized actors and use every trick in the book (and a few not) to make them appear the appropriate size. These techniques included:

Different Sized Props: Props for actors needing to appear small were made larger than duplicate smaller versions for actors needing to appear bigger.

Forced Perspective: Some actors were filmed farther from the camera than they appear, resulting in the illusion that they are smaller.

Scale Compositing: Actors were filmed separately, sometimes in differently scaled sets, and the separate pieces of film were composited together.

Scale Doubles: The lead hobbit actors sometimes shared their scenes with "Tall" Paul Randall playing the parts of Gandalf, Aragorn, or others — including Arwen! Standing over seven feet tall, Randall made the hobbit actors appear smaller. The lead actors who played Gandalf and the other big folk sometimes shared the stage with diminutive actors Praphaphorn Chansantor, Kiran Shah, Bhoja Kannada, Martin Gay, Trevor Bau, and Brett Beattie, creating the opposite effect. Sometimes a scene would even start with a scale double and end with the lead actor in his or her place after they subtly switched.

Platforms: In truth, the doubles were not directly proportionate to the lead actors. Randall, for example, had longer legs than the average-sized guys, but his shoulders were about the same width. Therefore, if one of the big folk wasn't walking, the lead actor on a platform worked out just as well as using a scale double.

Kneeling: The hobbit and dwarf actors kneeling worked out well too, if they didn't have to move in the scene.

Big Rigs: Stilt walkers wore oversized costumes with large, false remote-controlled arms. This technique did not work very well and was only used in the foreground or background of a few scenes with hobbits.

Digital Doubles: Rather than real actors, sometimes a shot had computer generated characters. This technique, the offspring of animation, solved the scale issue quite neatly.

Baker shares his September 22 birthday with Bilbo and Frodo. It is also, of course, the date of the long-expected party, which follows the prologue.

All three films used a new computer software package to create and animate armies of Orcs, Elves, and Men in battle — each figure possessing artificial intelligence. While this saved on the cost of extras, in the early simulations, about one-third of these digital creations ran away from the battle to avoid being killed. The programmers realized they had to add a bit of artificial stupidity.

Elendil, Isildur's father, was played by Peter McKenzie. McKenzie's son Bret appears later in the film and in *The Return of the King* as the Elf "Figwit" (see page 142).

The prologue was cut from the film, only to be reinstated just prior to the film's release.

What the Elvish Eyes and Ears Have Noticed

In 2001 and 2002, this film was usually referred to as *The Lord of the Rings* by New Line Cinema, theaters, and fans alike. It wasn't until the second film came out that *The Fellowship of the Ring* became its favored title.

The theatrical cut is sometimes called "Frodocentric" because of how many scenes seem to revolve around Frodo. The truth, however, is that the film is "One Ring–centric." It's the only movie based on a Tolkien book, animated or live-action, to be told almost completely from the Ring's point of view.

The Foolishness of a Took

When New Line Cinema registered its official *Lord of the Rings* website with Yahoo.com, the studio got the title of the first film wrong, identifying it as "The Fellowship of the Rings."

Galadriel tells us the Great Rings were forged, but the footage shows them being cast.

Isildur floats in the river, despite wearing about eighty pounds of armor.

Curiously, the filmmakers went to a great deal of effort to make Ian Holm appear younger when finding the Ring. Why is this necessary if Bilbo, as we'll learn, "hasn't aged a day" when Gandalf visits him at Bag End?

Hobbiton

Bilbo throws an extravagant birthday party and gives the Ring to Frodo. However, Gandalf discovers it is evil. Meanwhile, its creator, Sauron, learns where it is and sends his servants to reclaim it.

The picturesque home of the Hobbits. (Tom Wuellette)

What the Big Folk Were Saying

"They must have rounded up every short person in the world for this."
— A man as Hobbiton is shown

"Why aren't they wearing shoes?"
— Several moms when the Hobbits are introduced

"You said they couldn't do magic!"
— A nonfantasy fan to her husband, as Bilbo puts the Ring on

What the Wizards Know

George Lucas has cited *The Lord of the Rings* as an influence for *Star Wars*. At one point, Luke Skywalker and his Tatooine family were going to be Hobbit-sized. This idea changed, but Lucas did create his own "Hobbit" village in *Willow*, a 1988 fantasy film starring 3' 6" Warwick Davis.

The switch in studios delayed the start of *Fellowship of the Ring* shooting, allowing the vegetation in Hobbiton to mature and adding to the illusion that Hobbits had lived there for hundreds of years.

Jackson was hoping to find two unknown English actors to play Frodo and Sam.

Elijah Wood (Frodo) made his own audition tape, filming three scenes in a makeshift Hobbit costume, editing them together, and delivering the video to the casting director in Los Angeles.

Sean Astin attended two auditions for the part of Sam. He was cast after assuring Jackson that he'd have no trouble gaining weight for the part. His father, John Astin (best known for Gomez Addams of *The Addams Family*), auditioned for the part of Gandalf but was not as fortunate.

No piece of wardrobe concerned the filmmakers more than Gandalf's iconic hat; it was something that was easy for Tolkien to write but not easy to have in three dimensions in the films without looking silly or absurd. Jackson, knowing fans would be disappointed if it wasn't present, approved a design based on John Howe's *Gandalf the Grey* painting. But that didn't stop the cast and crew from looking for ways to "lose" it somewhere in the story!

When Ian Holm, who beat out Sylvester McCoy for the part of Bilbo, arrived in New Zealand, the Hobbiton set no longer existed. Jackson had filmed the needed scenes without Holm. Jackson had the Hobbit composited into the earlier footage through blue screen work.

Students in film school often begin their studies by examining the works of famous artists before moving onto films because painting is, in a way, the grandfather of filmmaking. Long before filmmakers had to figure out how to use lighting, framing, and perspective to bring a subject to life, or how to create a look and feel for a scene, painters were experimenting with the same properties the movies would use to bring their creations to life. Jackson, a savvy filmmaker, wisely studied many paintings of Middle-earth at the very beginning of this project. Many influenced these films. Bag End, at Jackson's request, was designed to look exactly like *Bilbo's Front Hall*, a 1995 painting by John Howe.

Tolkien was fortunate that he did not have to worry about how to frame his characters on screen. Finding a proper way to have characters of different heights in the same shot is always a challenge, which is why many films try to cast actors of a similar size. You can imagine the unique challenge presented to the directors of the films based on Tolkien's books!

The film wastes no time in giving us a complex scale trick: Gandalf handing his hat and staff to Bilbo. Sir Ian McKellen (Gandalf) and Ian Holm were filmed separately for this. McKellen handed his regular hat and staff to a stagehand in a small Bag End set, and another stagehand passed an oversized hat and staff to Holm in an oversized set. A computer combined the footage, taking out the stagehands, leaving in the actors, and giving us the illusion that these characters really can do anything with each other.

In the shot where Bilbo talks about mountains and then remembers to pour Gandalf some tea, the camera follows Bilbo around. This is a forced perspective shot, with Holm farther away from the camera than he appears. Normally, the camera moving would give away this two-dimensional trick. However, McKellen and part of the table were both rigged onto a platform, and as the camera moved, this platform (with McKellen and his half of the table) moved as well to preserve the illusion. The same trick is used again when Frodo pours Gandalf some tea. These complex tricks were done early to take our minds off the scale issues. If we as an audience begin to accept that the characters in a story not only can interact in any way, but can be filmed in any way as well, we stop focusing on the tricks and begin to focus on the story.

McKellen was supposed to join the cast at the beginning of the shoot, but delays in *Mission Impossible 2* (2000) led to further delays in McKellen's *X-Men* (2000), which forced *The Lord of the Rings*

Sir Ian McKellen joined the shoot late, but he did arrive precisely when he meant to. (Ian Smith)

crew to shoot McKellen-less scenes for the first few months while the actor finished up his work with mutants.

Tolkien described Bag End as looking westward, but the set actually faced east. To disguise this, Jackson cleverly had the "sunset" scene shot at sunrise.

The filmmakers ran into legal issues pertaining to *The Hobbit* before making *The Lord of the Rings*, but that did not stop them from using Tolkien's first book when making these films. For example, they found better descriptions of Bilbo and Bag End in *The Hobbit* than in *The Lord of the Rings*, and incorporated the details into these films.

The "long expected party" was not shot at the Hobbiton location. It was actually filmed inside a studio.

The party was shot before Howard Shore had been selected as the films' composer. To give the actors music to dance to, some local musicians, collectively called Plan 9, were brought in. It was assumed that their song, entitled "Flaming Red Hair," would be replaced when the "professional" guy came aboard, but Shore enjoyed their performance so much he kept it in the film.

Before shooting began, the lead actors took part in a six-week "boot camp" where they were trained in archery, horseback riding, boating, use of swords, speaking English with the correct dialect, speaking fictional languages with the correct dialect, and whatever else their particular parts called for. Wood and Astin's training included dancing.

Some of the early tests for the fireworks dragon looked incredible, but visual effects director Christian Rivers asked that the effect not look too complicated or superfluous, and it was redone in a more simplistic way. The digital animation for all three films followed this lead, serving the film, but not calling attention to itself.

Jackson included a shot of Odo Proudfoot shouting "Proudfeet!" as an homage to the animated *Lord of the Rings*, framing the shot the same way as Bakshi did.

The filmmakers thought about identifying locations such as Minas Tirith (where Gandalf discovers the Account of Isildur) with captions, but decided against it for fear it would look silly.

The portraits of Bilbo's parents, hanging above the fireplace in Bag End, are based on the likenesses of Jackson and Walsh.

Jackson spent so much time at the Bag End set, he fell in love with it and couldn't bear seeing it destroyed. He asked New Line Cinema if he could have it, and the studio said yes. This proved fortunate, because it allowed Jackson to conduct pick-up shots (extra shooting after the main shooting has been completed) in Bag End for *The Return of the King*. After that, the set was reassembled inside a hill at Jackson's country home — with additional designs by Alan Lee to make it three-dimensional and functional.

What the Elvish Eyes and Ears Have Noticed

Gandalf's first staff holds the wizard's pipe and tobacco.

When Gandalf visits Bag End, there's a framed map on the table, which he picks up and examines. This is Thrór's Map from *The Hobbit*, which Gandalf himself recovered from Sauron's dungeons 151 years earlier.

Merry first appears in the film just after Bilbo's party begins; he dances in front of the Hobbits carrying the cake, leading the way. Meanwhile, Pippin is playing in the band.

Billy and Katie Jackson, the children of Peter Jackson and Fran Walsh, appear in all three live-action *Lord of the Rings* films. In this film they can be seen listening to Bilbo's Troll story, along with the daughter of one of my interview subjects.

As Bilbo struggles to give up the Ring, the music probably sounds familiar to you, especially if you're in a choir or play an instrument. It's a descending broken third, commonly used by choruses and orchestras for practices and warm-ups. This motif is the "evil" theme for the first half of the film. (Choir warm-ups will never be the same again.)

At this point, Sauron's tower of Barad-dûr is still under construction and is nowhere near as impressive as it will be later in the trilogy.

When the mountains of Mordor are shown early in the film, you can see Osgiliath just beside them.

Notice Gandalf, watching Frodo shove everything into his bag haphazardly, neatly fold a shirt and hold it out to Frodo — who snatches it, lets it unfold, and shoves it into his bag again haphazardly.

The Foolishness of a Took

When Gandalf makes his big-screen debut, he dazzles us with his magic right away just to show us he's a wizard. As he drives into Hobbiton, his silver scarf is hanging on the right and his staff is on the left. In the next shot, the scarf and staff have switched sides. It's as if some film editor flipped the first shot to get the bend in the road to match the curve as Gandalf approaches Frodo.

There's a rumor that McKellen did not mean for Gandalf to hit his head on the rafters of Bag End and that it was an accident. McKellen, however, has since set the record straight: it was intentional.

Just before Bilbo pours Gandalf some tea, McKellen bumps the forced perspective table with his knees, revealing that his half is not connected to Bilbo's half.

As the Nazgûl approaches the hobbit to inquire about "Shire" and "Baggins," the supposedly frightened dog wags his tail.

As Frodo, Wood's English accent is usually very good, but "You've only just arrived" sounds more like a lad from Iowa than from the Shire.

The Ring Goes East

While Gandalf is imprisoned by the traitor Saruman, Frodo and his companions journey east, pursued by Sauron's servants. At Amon Sûl (Weathertop), the servants wound Frodo, but are forced to retreat. Frodo is quickly taken to Rivendell, where it is hoped he can be healed.

This limestone hill at Port Waikato served as Weathertop. (Rosi Waris)

What the Big Folk Were Saying

"Haha, he turned him into a horse!"

— A confused man after Gandalf says he's thought of a better use for Sam and the next shot has the wizard leading a horse and saying, "Come along, Samwise. Keep up!"

What the Wizards Know

The original idea was that only the good guys were going to ride horses, and the Nazgûl were going to ride creatures created specifically for this film. However, it was easier to deal with horses, so the filmmakers stuck with Tolkien's vision. They did have to digitally darken some parts of the Black Riders' horses, such as white ankles, so they would appear all black.

In the extended edition, the music for the Elvish procession entitled "The Elvish Lament" was composed and performed by Plan 9.

The lyrics are an Elvish translation of the very song Tolkien gives these Elves in the book.

Some of the miniature towers were so large, they couldn't fit under the overhead electrical cables when they were transported. Weta workers, wearing rubber gloves and rubber-soled boots, used long poles to lift the cables while the trucks drove under.

Orthanc was designed to look exactly like a 1989 painting by Alan Lee, also called *Orthanc*.

Sir Christopher Lee, a fan of the books when they were first published, once met Tolkien in an English pub. Lee auditioned for the part of Gandalf, his dream role. But at nearly eighty, he was thought to be too old for a part that required a surprising

Film veteran Sir Christopher Lee, who had read The Lord of the Rings *dozens of times over the years, served as an emissary of the fans.* (Jackson Lee/ AdMedia/ Keystone Press)

amount of stamina; Gandalf is constantly riding, fighting, and on the move. Lee's talents were perfect, however, for Saruman.

Want to be a wizard? Better get a new nose. Both McKellen and Lee wear prosthetic noses throughout the trilogy. All Gandalf's hair and that big hat tended to dwarf McKellen's natural features, so he wore a larger nose. Lee was given was given a slightly hooked nose to make his face more bitter and pinched.

Shore used 100 singers with a 100-piece orchestra for the wizards' duel.

Boyd was going to play Pippin with an English accent, but the Scottish accent fit the character better. Indeed, in Tolkien's *The Return of the King*, various people of Minas Tirith comment that Pippin has a strange accent.

Bakshi's idea of the Hobbits hiding under the roots of a tree as the Nazgûl looks for them was one of the best inventions of his film. The next decade, a young artist named John Howe borrowed the idea for one of his first professional paintings. A decade after that Jackson brought Howe aboard as conceptual artist for his film project and wanted an adaptation of the painting in his film. So the end result is Jackson's interpretation of Howe's interpretation of Bakshi's interpretation of Tolkien. The scene is wonderful in its own right, and works as a double homage: a tribute to both Bakshi and Howe at once. And that's certainly fitting — for it was Bakshi's film that introduced Jackson to *The Lord of the Rings*, and Howe's paintings that shaped how Jackson saw Middle-earth.

The heavy Nazgûl costumes included so many layers the actors had to wear about fifty meters of fabric.

Jackson was a bit disappointed with the look of the Nazgûl, preferring the computer-generated inky-black look of the Reaper in *The Frighteners*. He considered using the same effect for the Nazgûl, but there were too many of them and too many shots for that to happen.

"Shire . . . breakfast?" One of the Nazgûl, hopelessly lost in his search for Frodo. (Seth Daire)

The screams of the Nazgûl were changed shortly before the film was released. Concerned that they weren't scary enough, writer Fran Walsh visited the sound department and had her own screams recorded. These screams can be heard in all three films.

At this point in the movie, the filmmakers have used some complex tricks to sell the scale issue and it is now off our minds. This means they can pull back and use simpler tricks: such as having Dominic Monaghan (Merry) on his knees as the Hobbits enter Bree, allowing him to turn and face the camera while Frodo, Sam, and Pippin (played by scale doubles) are up ahead with the Gatekeeper of Bree.

The buildings of Bree were inspired by sixteenth-century English architecture. Five-hundred-year-old buildings at Exeter, where Tolkien went to school, were used as guides.

Most of the New Line Cinema promotional materials referred to Aragorn as "Strider" before the first film was released.

When Tolkien brought Strider into the story, he had no idea where he was going with the character. He simply wanted a mysterious stranger to add some tension. (He even toyed with the idea of the character eventually being revealed as Bilbo.) In the end, Tolkien took a page out of *The Hobbit*, giving his new creation Thorin's "Return of the King" act.

Like Wood, Vin Diesel submitted his own audition tape, hoping to land the part of Aragorn. Unlike Wood, he was not cast.

Viggo Mortensen (Strider/Aragorn) himself composed "The Lay of Beren and Luthien," the song that Aragorn sings in the extended edition on the way to Amon Sûl. It was the last scene to be deleted from the theatrical cut.

The *palantír* was made of wood and covered with a special wax.

Frodo's *mithril* shirt proved to be more than a prop. When the Nazgûl was filmed stabbing Frodo at Amon Sûl, Wood wore it under his costume for protection.

To give the films a romantic couple that would resonate with younger filmgoers, twenty-six-year-old Stuart Townsend and twenty-two-year-old Liv Tyler were cast as Aragorn and Arwen. Both were to be swashbuckling roles, reminiscent of Hercules and Xena, previously New Zealand's most famous exports. But when the actors learned about their characters, they started to have reservations about how their parts were written. Tyler thought Arwen did not need to fight to appear strong, or appear in so many scenes to be a major character. Townsend didn't believe Aragorn should be so young or so small (about 5' 9"), and he didn't know what he could do to fix the problem. Ultimately, these issues were addressed in separate ways.

For the shots of Amon Sûl (Weathertop), the filmmakers discovered a rather funky looking hill and decided to use it, even though it differed considerably from the book's description. The ruins on top were digitally composited.

Florian (left) played Asfaloth, Arwen's horse, and Jane Abbott (right) rode him as Liv Tyler's riding double. (Tom Wuellette)

Three days into shooting, Jackson, who had cast Townsend as Aragorn despite objections from New Line, realized the actor was not suitable for the part. Townsend, who had attended the "boot camp" and spent nearly two months preparing for his part and bonding with his cast mates, was released from the project.

After Townsend's release, Russell Crowe was asked if he was interested in playing the Ranger, but he declined.

Viggo Mortensen was originally considered for Aragorn, but initially lost out to Jackson's choice of Townsend. Mortensen did accept the part and was in New Zealand ready to go shortly after Townsend's release. Because shooting was already underway, Mortensen had to jump into the films (starting with scenes at Amon Sûl) without any of the training the others had, yet his character had to be the best horseman, sword master, and linguist in the trilogy.

The Nazgûl on their horses were played by some of New Zealand's best riders: mostly women in their forties and fifties.

The Orc blacksmiths beneath Isengard were played by the Weta workshop staff who made the weapons for the film.

Lurtz, the Uruk-hai captain, was played by stuntman Lawrence Makoare, who has fourteen older siblings. It took eleven hours for his makeup to be applied for the birthing scene.

What the Elvish Eyes and Ears Have Noticed
On the quest to Mount Doom, Frodo and Sam always travel left to right.

Composer Howard Shore slowly builds up the "Fellowship" musical theme throughout the first half of the film as the group is formed.

The book the first film is based upon doesn't have as much grand architecture as the latter two. There's Rivendell and Lothlórien, as well as some ancient ruins here and there, but that's about it. The filmmakers, therefore, borrowed some of the great places from the second and third books and worked them into the first film: Barad-dûr, Minas Tirith, Minas Morgul, and Isengard all make early appearances. With Edoras, Helm's Deep, Cirith Ungol, and much more of Gondor still to come, it was a sensible idea.

Frodo is the oldest of the four Hobbits, and Pippin is the youngest. Meanwhile, Billy Boyd (Pippin) is the oldest of the actors, and Wood is the youngest.

Just to add to his creepiness, when the horse-riding Nazgûl approaches the Hobbits for the first time, his approach is invisible until he appears from behind the tree.

The scriptwriters wisely skipped over several chapters of the book between Hobbiton and Bree. The book sets up a great deal of exposition about the Ring and the free peoples versus Sauron, then gives Frodo a series of leisurely adventures having nothing to do with any of that, and having little importance to the overall story before getting back on track. There's nothing wrong with doing this in a book. However, in a film, where time is precious, and the audience can't reread details, you can't get away with this. (Sorry, Tom Bombadil!)

Jackson has a cameo as "Albert Dreary," the drunken, carrot chomping man of Bree. Originally Dreary was to have a pipe, but it made Jackson feel ill, so he switched to a carrot.

While Jackson's and Bakshi's films are different in style, both cover *The Fellowship of the Ring* using a similar structure. They each begin with a prologue and include and omit the same basic parts of the book. Another similarity is that both show the Nazgûl attacking the Prancing Pony. In the book, the attack is the work of men of Bree.

In the book, Gandalf explains the history of the Nazgûl. The film does something more fitting: the lost King of Gondor explains what happened to the ancient Kings of old.

Notice that when the Hobbits and the Fellowship are in difficult environments, such as the Midgewater Marshes in the extended edition, Bill the Pony seems to be just out of frame in the close-ups. That's because a real pony couldn't be used in these locations, and the pantomime pony (with two actors playing the front and back) wasn't realistic enough for anything except wide shots.

Tolkien could only *show* us the languages he invented in his books. Finally, with these films, we can hear them, and realize how beautiful they really are.

Aragorn's song in the extended edition translates to: "Tinúviel the Elven fair, immortal maiden Elven-wise. About him cast her shadowy hair and arms like silver glimmering."

The sword Elrond uses in the prologue is the same sword Arwen uses to defy the Nazgûl at the Ford of Rivendell thousands of years later.

The theatrical cut of this film has far greater pacing in the first half than the extended edition. The filmmakers deserve great credit for making the cuts they did. Had they not done so, this film would not have sparked such a phenomenon.

From Hobbiton to Mordor
Creating Middle-earth

As important as Gandalf, Frodo, and the rest of the Fellowship are, Jackson and his people knew Middle-earth was just as important a character to Tolkien and needed to come alive for the films to succeed. To create the places of Middle-earth, various methods were used, sometimes in concert with each other.

Studio Sets: These environments, designed, built, painted, and dressed for their specific scenes, had the advantage of stability. The filmmakers knew exactly what they were going to get here. An example of a scene filmed this way is the attack at Amon Sûl (Weathertop).

Locations: Scouts searched New Zealand for real environments where sets could be built. For example, they found a farm that turned out to be the perfect spot for Hobbiton.

Matte Paintings: Artists designed backdrops for the films. Because of digital technology, many of these paintings were animated and/or virtually three dimensional, making them more alive and versatile than previously possible.

Miniatures: When it was too expensive to build a full-size set, scale models were used. Sometimes they were even used on set in the background. Building a model was cheaper, but presented new challenges. The doors of the Minas Tirith model, for example, had to match the full-size doors on set, and yet a much smaller surface was available for decorating.

Virtual Sets: Sometimes a set existed only in a computer, and the actors were filmed in front of a blue or green screen. An example of this is Dwarrowdelf, which was too expansive to do as a miniature.

Digital Compositing: Computer technology enabled the filmmakers to assemble the separate techniques and multiple images into a final image, allowing for a combination of methods and enhanced sets. The waterfalls of Rivendell, for example, were not part of the miniature or set, but were photographed in other parts of New Zealand, then composited into the scenes.

The Foolishness of a Took

The Hobbit actors decided to have some fun with us at the Prancing Pony. Just before Frodo asks Butterbur who Strider is, Pippin heads to the bar to get a pint. As Frodo talks to Butterbur, only three Hobbits remain at the table, as you might expect — except instead of the three being Frodo, Sam, and Merry, they are Frodo, Sam, and *Pippin!*

Speaking of the Prancing Pony, how do the Nazgûl find out which room Frodo is *supposed* to be in? Do they check with the front desk before going on their stabbing spree? (Now I have this image in my head of Witch-king of Angmar politely ringing the bell in the lobby while the rest of the Nazgûl look up into the air and try to appear inconspicuous.)

After the Hobbits ask Strider where he is taking them, he answers, "Into the wild" and then walks right into the camera, bumping it. Jackson sure knows how to make us feel like we're right there with the characters — sometimes we even get in their way.

In the extended edition, as Pippin slips and falls down in the Midgewater Marshes, Boyd's prosthetic foot begins to slip off. (Boyd also had issues with his prosthetic ears, but you can hardly notice. Early in the shoot, the ears had a tendency to fill with air, making him look like Dumbo. The early footage was edited to disguise this problem, and the ears were redesigned for the remainder of the shoot.)

The Witch-king of Angmar draws his sword twice as he approaches Frodo at Amon Sûl.

When Arwen appears for the first time and dismounts from Asfaloth, she has a different hairstyle and is wearing a different dress than in subsequent shots.

Those Nazgûl are quick with their hands at the Ford! After drawing their swords with their left hands, in the second the camera cuts away for a closeup of their horses, they all switch their swords to their right hands.

In the December 15, 2001, issue of *TV Guide*, a photo of Frodo and Arwen appeared, with the caption identifying the actors as Wood and Tyler. Actually, Frodo in the picture was not Wood, who would be the wrong scale, but a dummy.

Rivendell

Frodo awakens to find he and his friends are safe. Meanwhile, Aragorn and Arwen discuss their future. A Council is held to decide what to do with the Ring, and Frodo agrees to bear it to Mount Doom.

Spectacular Kaitoke Regional Park served as Rivendell.

(Diane Rooney)

What the Big Folk Were Saying

". . . Mr. Anderson."

— A man finishing Elrond's line when he says to Frodo, "Welcome to Rivendell . . . "

"Cause I'm outta here."

— A woman finishing Elrond's line after he says, "One of you must do this . . ."

What the Wizards Know

One day while shooting Rivendell, Jackson was so tired he caught a couple hours of sleep in Frodo's bed.

Film scouts looked for the ideal location for Rivendell but never did find it; Jackson settled for sets built at Kaitoke Regional Park, supplementing them with miniatures, matte paintings, and digital compositing.

Ed Mulholland, construction supervisor, said Rivendell was the most difficult of the sets to build.

Millions of silk leaves were imported from China for the scenes with the Elves to give a feeling of Autumn to the departing race.

On the Rivendell set, Astin was hit on the head by an Elven loom and had to get a computed axial tomography (CAT) scan.

The dialogue between Elrond and Isildur had to be redubbed because of background noise on set. Because Isildur says only one word in the trilogy ("no"), it wasn't worth bringing actor Harry Sinclair (Isildur) back. Instead, Hugo Weaving (Elrond) talks to himself. While rerecording Elrond's dialogue, he also voiced Isildur's "no."

In a 1990s British television miniseries Sean Bean (Boromir) played a Napoleonic-era army officer known as Richard Sharpe. He subsequently appeared in commercials where he would allude to his earlier role, saying things like, "Sharpe idea." After touching the shards of Narsil in this film, he continues the joke.

In early drafts of the screenplay, Boromir referred to himself in the third person as "Old Boromir."

The song that serves as the score for Aragorn and Arwen's romantic moment on the bridge was written, composed, and performed by Enya. It is entitled, "Aníron" which is Elvish for "I Desire." Its lyrics translate to: "From darkness I understand the night: dreams flow, a star shines. Ah! I desire Evenstar. Look! A star rises out of the darkness. The song of the star enchants my heart. Ah! I desire . . ."

Many different "One Rings" were made for the trilogy, partly because of scale issues and partly because large Rings — the size of dinner plates — were necessary for close-ups.

John Rhys-Davies required four and a half hours of makeup for the part of Gimli.

Wood, Astin, and Monaghan, after a long day's work. (Ian Smith)

The scriptwriters struggled mightily with the Council of Elrond. The climax proved especially challenging. It was Astin who ultimately came up with the idea that Frodo should volunteer to take the Ring while everyone is shouting. Astin also thought it was important that Sam be at the Council. (He's there in the book, and in the remainder of the story Sam seems to have a clear understanding of what happened at the Council.) The plan was then changed from excluding him, to including all the Hobbits, with Sam, Merry, and Pippin hiding in the background until the end.

The actors were given personalized chairs to sit in during the shoot. However, the names on the chairs were not, "Ian McKellen," "Elijah Wood," or "Orlando Bloom," but rather "Gandalf," "Frodo," "Legolas," etc.

When Weta designed the silicon puppet of Bilbo turned into Gollum (which was blended into Holm's face in post-production for Bilbo's brief transformation), it was a key moment in Gollum's development. Weta learned Gollum's look could be most effective if he was modeled after a real actor. (Meanwhile, Holm loved the puppet so much, Weta gave him a bronze version of it as a parting gift.)

What the Elvish Eyes and Ears Have Noticed

Elrond's first lines in Elvish are not subtitled. However, audience members with good memories will understand him. He speaks the same words that Arwen spoke to Frodo earlier: "Hear my voice. Come back to the light."

Orlando Bloom plays Legolas with such ease, most people don't realize what a demanding part it is. Bloom's Legolas is a combination of earnestness and maturity that simultaneously creates a sense of youthfulness and immortality perfect for the Elvish Prince whom Tolkien describes in mostly abstract terms.

Orlando Bloom was discovered by Peter Jackson when Bloom was finishing school in England. (Ian Smith)

In addition to Narsil, we can see two other important weapons in the Grand Chamber of Rivendell. Aiglos, the spear of Gilgalad (the Elven-king in the prologue), is leaning next to the mural, *Aftermath of Battle*, which represents the living, after Sauron's defeat, searching the battlefield for loved ones. It's easy to imagine Elrond placing the spear there in memory. Hadhafang, the sword used by both Elrond and Arwen, is also present. Arwen must have taken it from this chamber, then returned it.

Whenever Aragorn has a romantic scene with Arwen, he strokes her ears. He must have an Elvish ear fetish. (Look out, Legolas!)

At the Council of Elrond, the Gondor theme mournfully plays as Boromir talks about his homeland. As it's played subtly by a single instrument, it's easy to overlook. Yet it's the same theme that dramatically plays in the extended edition of *The Two Towers* as Boromir declares Osgiliath reclaimed. The theme is also a key part of *The Return of the King*, majestically playing as Gandalf and Pippin enter Minas Tirith, and perhaps even more memorably playing as the beacons speed their fire westward.

Gimli breaks his axe trying to destroy the Ring. When he offers his services to Frodo, he grabs the axe belonging to the dwarf to his left. Apparently he's not giving it back, as he says, "And *my* axe."

The Foolishness of a Took
Sam must have been so worried about Mr. Frodo's wound that he lost his appetite. When Sam talks to Frodo about preparing to leave Rivendell for home, he's noticeably thinner. (That's because this was a pickup scene shot after Astin had lost some weight.)

When Arwen and Aragorn are alone together on a bridge of Rivendell, in the beginning Arwen moves her lips as Aragorn's voice is heard.

Sauron gave the One Ring some interesting powers. At the Council of Elrond, there is a closeup of it while everyone argues. Curiously, the Ring's reflection of the Council's participants is the same as

The ever classy John Rhys-Davies. (Daryl Simr)

the reality and not a mirror image. No doubt Sauron intended to use this power to help subdue the Free Peoples of Middle-earth.

Rhys-Davies is missing the end of his middle finger on his left hand due to a farming accident as a child. The makeup artists made artificial, gelatin fingertips for him to wear in the films. (The

The Fellowship of the Ring Easter Egg Alert

There is an Easter egg hidden in *The Fellowship of the Ring* Platinum Series Special Extended Edition (the four disc set that comes in a green box). It is not suitable for children and not included in some regions with strict standards. For regions such as North America where it is included, on the first disc you can access the MTV Movie Awards parody of the Council of Elrond starring Jack Black and Sarah Michelle Gellar. Simply go to the "Select a Scene" menu and navigate to the final group of scenes. Then navigate down from Scene 27 to reveal a hidden Ring symbol and press "Enter."

original *Star Trek* did a similar thing with the actor who played Scotty.) This puzzles me. Wouldn't it make sense for a battle hardened dwarf and a chief engineer of a Starship to be missing parts?

The Mountains

Frodo and his companions attempt to climb over the mountains barring their way, but fail. Instead, they journey through the mountains via a secret underground Dwarvish realm. There they are attacked several times, and Gandalf falls while the others escape.

The mountains prove a difficult barrier for the new Fellowship to cross. (Diane Rooney)

What the Big Folk Were Saying

"Don't they brush their teeth? That's so unattractive."
— A woman commenting on the Orcs

"Not again!"
— A young girl when the cave troll hits Frodo with his spear

"He's a Transformer."
— A boy when Gandalf says Frodo is more than meets the eye

"Dude, the old geezer's gone!"
— A teenager to his friends as Gandalf falls

What the Wizards Know

When the cast were trained in sword fighting, they were taught to remember each position as a number. They could then be told a

Sean Bean (Boromir) is loved by his fans, who call themselves Beanstalkers. (Kathy Hutchins/ Zuma Press/ Keystone Press)

sequence of numbers and they'd know what to do. When Sean Bean (Boromir) was given a scene where his character teaches the Hobbits how to use their swords, he simply used these numbers. (Gondor must have a similar system.)

With a population of about 6000, a small town in Manitoba, Canada, wouldn't seem likely to draw much attention. When you consider the town's name is Gimli, however, you can understand why some people suddenly took interest in it around the year 2001.

The same material could not be used for the different sized costumes the actors and their scale doubles wore. Had this been done, the material would not have appeared to fold or move in a consistent way. Therefore, the costumes weren't just made in different scales, the raw material for them (woven from different scaled looms) varied as well.

The location for the Doors of Moria was a dammed up, flooded parking lot.

John Rhys-Davies (Gimli) had an incredible amount of makeup and numerous prosthetics applied to his face to make him appear to be a different race. The actor's skin reacted badly to this, and soon he needed days off between shooting recover. While he was gone, a double took his place. Also, at 6' 1" Rhys-Davies was the tallest of the Fellowship actors, so his scale double was needed for most of the shots where other actors were present (although he was the right height to share scenes with the lead Hobbit actors). As a result, most of the time when you see Gimli throughout the three films, he is not being played by Rhys-Davies.

When Jackson began editing *Bad Taste* (1987), his first serious project, he had a ten-minute film in mind. Imagine his surprise when he finished his first cut and it took an hour to watch it. Jackson loves to create elaborate sequences out of simple script instructions. In *The Fellowship of the Ring*, for example, a script comment about the Fellowship running down some stairs became a three-minute action event. In a bit of déjà vu, when *The Fellowship of the Ring* was in its editing phase, it was discovered to be much longer than the two hours and twenty minutes each of *The Lord of the Rings* films was supposed to be. Heavy editing brought it down to about three hours, and New Line Cinema agreed to this length, wisely noting that the sequels could be shorter (or even longer) depending upon the public's reaction to their first three hours in Middle-earth.

To get the film down to three hours, some moments that were important to the sequels had to be cut. This led to the idea of an extended edition DVD.

The score for Moria includes Dwarvish chants. To achieve them, Shore directed a chorus of sixty male Maori vocalists, fifty singers, and ten rugby players.

Tolkien was going to have an Orc archer wound Legolas in Moria but reconsidered.

Perhaps no part of the trilogy was more important to the commercial success of the films than the Moria sequence. In May 2001 it served as the centerpiece of a twenty-five-minute preview shown at the Cannes Film Festival. Had journalists been less than impressed, it could have led to six months of negative publicity before the first film was released.

What the Elvish Eyes and Ears Have Noticed

Images of the Fellowship majestically striding through the mountains (reminding me of *The Sound of Music*) were used in the trilogy's teaser trailer and played in theaters in January 2001. This trailer included the title and year of release for each film. Coincidently, just as the words "*The Return of the King*" appeared, the film's title character, Aragorn, walked into the shot. Also interestingly, the credits at the end of the trailer included only the names New Line Cinema thought would put butts in seats. Unknown Orlando Bloom was not listed.

The ruins the Fellowship pass are clearly the remains of Ost-in-Edhil, a Second Age fortress of the Elves (ruled for a time by Galadriel) that was destroyed by Sauron.

Just as the camera rises over the rocks to show Merry and Pippin's sword fighting lessons, Merry returns a favor by tossing Aragorn an apple.

Legolas and Gandalf hardly seem to notice each other in this film.

Well before the first film was released, a picture of Boromir holding the Ring (on Caradhras) was published alongside articles about the films. It certainly caught the attention of the fans of the book, who didn't have any idea where this was or what was going on!

The talented and uncredited Ted Nasmith, seen here at a bookstore signing. (Danacea Ware)

As Boromir looks at the Ring, it appears to twitch. The viewer is left to decide whether it is simply a result of its interaction with the moving chain or something more sinister.

Many fans know that the paintings of conceptual artists Alan Lee and John Howe were inspirations for various places and scenes in these films. Paintings the two had worked on years before were used by Jackson as a guide in the early stages of the project, which is partly why he asked them to come aboard as conceptual artists. What you might not know is that Jackson also asked Ted Nasmith, the other famous Tolkien artist, to join the project as well. Nasmith was not available, but Jackson still used quite a few of his paintings as the basis for scenes throughout the film. The shot of the Fellowship dramatically walking along the ledge of Caradhras is nearly identical to Nasmith's painting *The Redhorn Pass*.

Most of the Elvish in the films is Sindarin, the common Elvish tongue. However, as Saruman tries to awaken Caradhras, he uses the more formal Elvish language of Quenya (Tolkien's favorite). Tolkien thought about writing all of *The Lord of the Rings* in Elvish, but worried it might hurt sales.

Throughout Frodo's quest the phases of the Moon are borrowed from the phases of the Moon in 1941 and 1942.

You can tell the filmmakers didn't really have a handle on Gollum's look at this point. His eyes, cheeks and forehead plane all change in the second film.

Alan Lee's painting *In the Halls of Moria* comes to life when the Fellowship visits the great realm and Dwarf city of Dwarrowdelf.

The way the light strikes Balin's Tomb, it looks like the image right out of *Citizen Kane* (1941) where Mr. Thompson visits Walter Thatcher's library. However, this is no homage. This perfectly matches Tolkien's description, which was written in the late 1930s.

Gandalf's oversized hat and staff, last handled by Holm, make another appearance: this time in the hands of Boyd as Pippin in Moria. Notice that unlike the exchange of these props between McKellen and Holm at Bag End, there's no need for fancy tricks by this time because our minds are focused on the story, not the scale issues. In Moria, McKellen hands his hat and staff to a scale double in one shot, Boyd holds the oversized versions in another shot, and the editor, not a computer, makes it seamless.

Whether due to budget cuts or to avoid confusion, Glamdring, the sword of Gandalf, doesn't glow blue in the presence of Orcs, as described in the books.

The cave-troll, from his life to his death, is reminiscent of (or a precursor to) King Kong.

As the Orcs prepare to scamper down on the Fellowship from above, everyone concentrates on the path ahead or the pursuit behind, save Legolas who has that sixth Elvish sense and looks up.

Shortly after the Fellowship is surrounded by Orcs, there's a close-up of one with large eyes. As Vance Hartwell, who did makeup for the film, will explain later in this book, all the Moria Orcs were going to have their eyes digitally enlarged like this, but the plan changed.

Well, I suppose Pippin feels extra sad exiting Moria in this adaptation considering he's pretty much solely responsible for Gandalf's death here.

As the Fellowship begins to break, so does the "Fellowship" musical theme.

The attacks on the World Trade Center and the Pentagon happened just three months before the release of this film. While any impact they had on the film industry is trivial compared to their impact on the victims, these attacks did come very close to changing the course of *The Lord of the Rings* film project. Had the attacks occurred closer to the *Fellowship of the Ring* release date, it's likely the distracted public would not have noticed the advertisements or glowing reviews for it. Following the attacks, most people were not in the mood for films anyway. Had *The Fellowship of the Ring* been out of theaters before it had a chance to find its audience, *The Two Towers* would have faced postproduction without pickup shots or much of a budget — and would likely have been edited down to about two hours. Had that film failed at the box office, it's possible *The Return of the King* (all ninety minutes of it) would have been released directly to DVD.

Instead, another scenario unfolded. Much like the people of the United States embracing the Beatles all the more when the band appeared on *The Ed Sullivan Show* a few months after the assassination of President Kennedy, the world, ready to move on by December 2001 and looking for something to help it heal, embraced *The Fellowship of the Ring* like a comforting friend. The film's themes resonated even more to a popular culture suddenly shocked out of its cynicism and love of antiheroes, and the phenomenon snowballed, with each new installment of the trilogy outgrossing its predecessor.

The Foolishness of a Took

The Hobbit actors decided to have some more fun with us. As Merry tosses stones into the evil water outside the Doors of Moria, Pippin is sitting calmly next to him. In the next shot, Pippin's on his feet throwing stones and Merry's sitting down.

Before Bakshi was brought onboard to direct *The Lord of the Rings* (1978), John Boorman (who corresponded with Tolkien) was spearheading the project. In Boorman's script (which was later discarded), Gimli cannot remember the password to Moria, so Gandalf forces him to dig a hole and crawl inside, then violently beats him. Gimli then recovers his memory of the ancient tongue and springs forth to speak the words needed to open the doors.

In the extended edition, as McKellen walks along the ledge (just before explaining what the mine is for), he kicks a wire that runs along the ground and up Gandalf's staff. And here you thought its light was magical. Good thing Moria has electrical outlets!

Why doesn't Frodo just drop the Ring into one of the deep chasms of Moria? (I know, I know, Gandalf would say it could be rediscovered in 20,000 years or something. Well, I would have taken the risk.)

Curiously, Frodo's sword Sting doesn't glow blue when the Fellowship is surrounded by all the Orcs of Moria. It probably figures, "Not even I can help you now, buddy."

When Miramax was trying to convince Jackson to do *The Lord of the Rings* as one film, the studio suggested the journey inside Moria didn't have to be shown if the Fellowship simply talked about how scary it was on their way to Lothlórien.

Lothlórien

The Companions seek shelter in the hidden Elvish realm of Lothlórien. Its ruler, Galadriel, gives them warnings and gifts, sending them on their way in boats.

Lothlórien is a place of healing with no evil in it, unless a man brings evil there with him. (Massimiliano Manni)

What the Big Folk Were Saying

"What's he gonna do with an Avon bottle?"
— A man as Frodo is given the phial of Galadriel

What the Wizards Know

Jackson shot the Fellowship meeting with the Elves of Lothlórien in two different ways. In the first, which appears in the theatrical cut, Haldir tells the Fellowship they have entered Lothlórien and must go before the Lady of the Wood. In the second, the Fellowship is chased into Lothlórien by the Moria Orcs, only to be rescued by the Elves who are then uncertain of what to do with Frodo since he carries a great evil. The extended edition uses a combination of both, using the beginning of the first and cutting to the Fellowship after being rescued in the second. (This is why Legolas says, "Our Fellowship stands in your debt.")

Howard Shore, the musical genius. (Ian Smith)

Craig Parker (Haldir) became involved with this production at its
earliest stages. He was cast as Frodo in a recorded version of the
script Jackson used for his storyboards. If you have the
Platinum Series Special Extended Edition, you can hear Parker,
as Frodo, narrating the prologue. It is on the first disc of the
Appendices, under "Visualizing the Story, Early Storyboards."
Jackson shared this recording with the cast to show them what
he had in mind.

The filmmakers added music, borrowed from other films, onto
these storyboards to give them an idea how everything was
working cinematically. While the Art Department had been
listening to the soundtracks of films such as *Braveheart* (1995)
and *The Last of the Mohicans* (1992) while they worked on their
designs, Jackson thought these scores were not subtle enough
for *The Lord of the Rings.* After some experimentation, Jackson
found that music from *The Silence of the Lambs* (1991), *Naked
Lunch* (1991), and *Crash* (1996) worked surprisingly well with
his storyboards. He then noticed that these compositions, as

well as others he thought appropriate, were all by the same person: Howard Shore. Shore, who had been a *Lord of the Rings* fan since he was a boy, was contacted. He gladly offered his services.

What do the Grand Chamber of Rivendell, the interior of Orthanc, and Galadriel's Glade have in common? The sets were all built at the same spot: Studio A.

Ngila Dickson, costume supervisor, found the Elven cloaks the most difficult costumes to create in terms of finding a material that was realistic but unrealistic at the same time.

Deadline pressure forced Dickson to create multiple designs for some of the main characters' costumes, so shooting wouldn't be delayed if Jackson didn't like how a design looked. The costumes that were made but not worn by the lead actors were used by the extras.

Those darn Elven cloaks forced the Costume Department to redesign the backpacks because of how the two pieces of gear interacted. This is another case where Tolkien could write whatever he wanted, but the filmmakers had to deal with reality. (Think about poor McKellen who originally had to carry around a scarf, a hat, a staff, and a sword wherever he went! No wonder he has Gandalf lose some items throughout the journey.) The packs in the film come up over the shoulders, fit under the arms and tie between the shoulder blades. The quiver of arrows carried by Legolas had to be tied in a complex way to keep it from bobbing around as well.

Monaghan was allergic to his Elven cloak.

When Jackson agreed to cut out the gift-giving scene from the theatrical cut, he made New Line Cinema promise to release the extended edition before *The Two Towers* — which shows some of the gifts in use — hit the theaters. This is why the extended edition was released in November 2002.

What the Elvish Eyes and Ears Have Noticed

So what does *Ishkhaqwi ai durugnul* (as Gimli says in the extended edition) mean? It loosely translates to: "I'll be in the third film, and guess who won't!" Alright, it really means, "I spit on your grave."

Aragorn's emphatic Elvish to Haldir in the extended edition, urging him to let Frodo into Caras Galadhon, translates to: "Please understand, we need your support! We need your protection! The road is very dangerous."

The lyrics for the "Lament for Gandalf" (which Legolas refuses to translate) are three verses about Gandalf coming from the West to guard Middle-earth, but departing too soon.

In the extended edition, when Sam recites his little poem about Gandalf's fireworks, he speaks of "silver showers." The scriptwriters must have thought that "golden showers," as it is in the book, might be taken the wrong way. (I didn't notice any outrage from the purists here.)

In the extended edition, Boromir tells Frodo that Gandalf would not want him to give up hope. He is being kind. A short time later, Boromir admits to Aragorn that it's been a long time since they had any hope.

Boromir says, "My father is a noble man." Interestingly, his father Denethor is played by John Noble.

"The Scouring of the Shire," a chapter about the Shire being overrun by thugs, would never make sense at the end of a film adaptation of *The Return of the King* unless a great deal of exposition was presented first. (And even then it would be anticlimactic.) It does, however, work well as a warning to Frodo in this first film. (And it's nice to see it somewhere.)

Sean Astin has said that filmmaking is a counterintuitive process, where actors are often forced to pretend the opposite of reality. (For example, if a scene takes place in the snow, it's usually

Academy Award winner Cate Blanchett. (Lisa O'Connor/ Zuma Press/ Keystone Press)

filmed in a hot studio.) These films take this axiom to a new level. We have Pippin, the youngest of the Hobbits by far, being played by an actor who is older than Cate Blanchett (Galadriel), the embodiment of an ancient Elf. And Blanchett, playing a character noted for being tall, only stands about 5' 8" while Gimli, noted for being short, is played by an actor who stands over six feet tall. Think about that one while Galadriel looks down upon Gimli!

Lady Galadriel's gift to Gimli in the extended edition is impressive, considering she refused the same request from Fëanor, one of the greatest Elves in Middle-earth history and creator of the *palantíri*.

This film has some interesting parallels with *The Wizard of Oz* (1939). Both were filmed about forty years after the books they were based upon were published. Each film is about a young orphan on a quest far away from home who gains companions along the way. Each film includes an homage to a somewhat unpopular previous attempt at a film adaptation (released in 1925 and 1978 respectively). While *Oz* was being shot, thirty-year-old Buddy Ebsen was replaced by forty-year-old Jack Haley as the Tin Man. While *Fellowship* was being shot, twenty-six-year-old Stuart Townsend was replaced by forty-one-year-old Viggo Mortensen as Aragorn. The Wizard, played by Frank Morgan, appears in *Oz* only briefly, but Morgan appears throughout the film in other roles. The Lord of the Rings, played by Sala Baker, appears only briefly in *The Fellowship of the Ring*, but Baker appears throughout the film in other roles as well. Finally, *The Wizard of Oz* was nominated for the Academy Award for Best Picture but lost to *Gone With the Wind* (1939), another adaptation of a book. *The Fellowship of the Ring* was nominated for an Academy Award for Best Picture but lost to *A Beautiful Mind* (2001), an adaptation of a book as well. In 2008, the American Film Institute named their top ten favorite fantasy films: *The Wizard of Oz* came in first, and *The Fellowship of the Ring* came in second.

The Foolishness of a Took

The *London Sunday Times* interviewed Blanchett in July 2000. Since the writer of the article didn't really know what this *Lord of the Rings* thing was all about, she did a quick search on the internet to get some info to fill out her piece. Thus her article said: "For the uninitiated, Galadriel is the good sister of the evil but beautiful Queen Beruthiel, who imprisons the Fellowship of the Ring in the forest of Lóthlorien. In the book, Galadriel frees them from her sister's clutches. It's a small but memorable part, and Blanchett lobbied hard for it." Kids, this is an example of why you shouldn't rely on the internet when you do book reports.

When the Fellowship is departing from Lothlórien and Galadriel is riding in her swan boat, a crew member makes an unscheduled cameo behind and to the left of the Elf.

The End of Some Things

At Amon Hen, Boromir, overcome with lust for power, attempts to take the Ring from Frodo, who flees. Meanwhile, the company is attacked by Orcs, led by Lurtz, their captain. Merry and Pippin are captured, Frodo and Sam escape, and Boromir is killed.

At Amon Hen, the Fellowship breaks. (Heather Cuthill)

What the Big Folk Were Saying

"Not him, you idiot! Take the ugly dwarf!"
— A young girl as Lurtz shoots arrows at Boromir

"Is that Kirsten Dunst?"
— Someone trying to see through Lurtz's makeup

"Did he borrow André the Giant's paddle or something?"
— Someone commenting on Frodo's paddle

"NO! You are NOT DOING this to me!"
— A young man as the film fades to black

"Well that was left open for a sequel."
— A woman to her husband as the film fades to black

What the Wizards Know

A set was built along a river in Queenstown for the scene where the Fellowship is attacked by Orcs on the Anduin River (as in the book). Unfortunately, before the scene was shot, extreme flooding washed the set away, and the sequence was abandoned.

Oddly enough, one of the worst accidents was sustained by conceptual artist Alan Lee. While examining the Amon Hen statue he tripped and broke his wrist. Fortunately, it wasn't his drawing arm.

The feathers for Legolas' arrows were from pheasants and turkeys. Gimli's beard was made from yak hair.

When Monaghan and Boyd were filmed throwing stones at the Uruk-hai (as seen in the extended edition), Boyd hit a cameraman and broke his nose.

While shooting the scene where Sam marches into the water (which was actually a freezing cold lake) to catch the departing Frodo, Astin badly cut his foot on . . . something. . . . (The object was never found, so nobody knows what it was.) He had to be flown to a hospital for stitches. Astin was back on set the next day, and, as a thank-you for his swift return, the film crew presented him with a Maori walking stick.

The version of this film formatted to fit the old 4:3 television screens, as expected, crops off the sides. However, you might be surprised to learn it includes more of the top and bottom of the picture than the 2.35:1 version you probably own. Too bad we can't combine them into a 16:9 ratio that fits the modern widescreen television.

When Harvey and Bob Weinstein, the founders and co-chairs of Miramax, sold *The Lord of the Rings* to New Line Cinema, the deal included Executive Producer credits for each of them at the end of each film.

Harvey Weinstein might be the most important person in the credits you don't know about. It's easy to say a book should be made into a film, but navigating through legal issues and getting the project underway is much more difficult. Weinstein, a fan of Tolkien, did just that. And when he was put between a rock and a hard place, Weinstein gave *The Lord of the Rings* a new home, where the project could continue to grow and meet its potential. Despite what happened with Miramax, we all owe Weinstein thanks for his vital part of the process of bringing Middle-earth to the world's cinemas.

Just two weeks prior to filming, the chief lighting technician quit because he thought he was too "professional" for this backwoods New Zealand project. Veteran gaffer Brian Bansgrove, who had worked on dozens of Australian films over the years, including *Gallipoli* (1981) and *Crocodile Dundee* (1986), was considered a risky choice for the job because of his age and health. Yet despite those who said his best days were behind him, he stepped in and proved everyone wrong. At sixty, Bansgrove, whose work appears throughout the trilogy, died just as *The Fellowship of the Ring* was becoming a hit at the box office. Director of photography Andrew Lesnie credited Bansgrove as the chief reason the film won the Oscar for Best Cinematography. The gaffer also inspired Sean Astin to create the short film, *The Long and Short of It* (2003), starring some of the cast and crew of *The Lord of the Rings*.

What the Elvish Eyes and Ears Have Noticed

Those clever filmmakers try to trick us on the river. The editing makes it appear as if Legolas and Lurtz nearly spot each other. However, knowing that each is going south, we can see they look both look the wrong way. As Lurtz growls, he looks right, which is west. Legolas then looks over his left shoulder, which is east. This is not a mistake, as Lurtz and Legolas do not actually see each other any more than the Hobbits are stabbed by the Nazgûl at the Prancing Pony. It is some creative editing though!

The Argonath statues along the Anduin River (representing the ancient border of Gondor) honor Isildur (left) and his father Elendil (right) from the prologue. The statues even have the

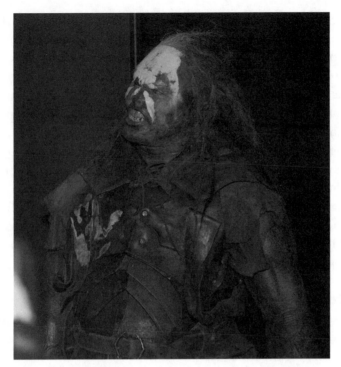

Lurtz (Lawrence Makoare), wondering why he keeps getting asked to Spider-Man conventions. (Ian Smith)

same helmets on their heads that their counterparts wore in their battle against Sauron.

It seems that when carving the Argonath, Gondor ran out of rock. Look closely and you'll see the top portions are made of stone blocks — and you can see the quarries the blocks came from to the right and left of the statues.

Did you notice Gimli describes the beginning of the next film, telling us exactly where Frodo and Sam will go?

Some of the ruins around this northern border of Gondor look suspiciously similar to the ones we saw at Amon Sûl.

As a sign that he is accepting his ancestry, Aragorn takes Boromir's gauntlets to wear for the remainder of the films.

The scriptwriters handled the end of the first film particularly well, with more coherency and less chaos than its counterpart in the books. In the text, Frodo and Sam have no idea there's an Orc attack, while Aragorn, Legolas, and Gimli do not know what happened to Sam and Frodo, but know some Hobbits have been captured (though not which ones), and Merry and Pippin have no idea that the rest of the company has divided. In this adaptation everyone's knowledge and decisions are crystal clear: Frodo says his goodbye to the Fellowship (to Aragorn), Merry and Pippin realize he's leaving and give themselves up so he can have a safe getaway, and Aragorn, Legolas, and Gimli realize they've done their part for Frodo and must attempt to rescue Merry and Pippin. These changes not only allow for a cleaner end to the first film, but a cleaner start to the second.

The Foolishness of a Took

In the extended edition, Aragorn says he won't lead the Ring to within one hundred leagues of Minas Tirith. That would take Mount Doom off the itinerary.

The Collector's DVD Gift Set came with little Argonath statues, sculpted by the film's visual effects artists, which are actually quite useful as bookends for the DVDs. However, the statues aren't quite as big as the television commercials in November 2002 implied. In these spots, while the narrator talks about these polystone figures, shots of the actual eight-foot Argonath miniatures under construction are shown. (Some poor eleven-year-old was probably disappointed when he opened the box and saw his figures were only six inches high.)

In the extended edition, when Legolas is shooting arrows with lightning speed at Amon Hen, the fifth Orc he kills begins his dramatic fall before the arrow reaches him.

In the fight between Aragorn and Lurtz, when Aragorn is thrown against a tree, he loses his sword. In the next shot, when Lurtz throws his shield at the Ranger, Aragorn . . . loses his sword again.

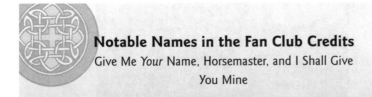

Notable Names in the Fan Club Credits
Give Me *Your* Name, Horsemaster, and I Shall Give You Mine

The names of the charter members of the Lord of the Rings Fan Club are included in the credits of the extended editions. Here is a selected list you might find interesting:

Bill Amend — cartoonist behind the nationally syndicated *FoxTrot* strip.

Billy Boyd and Dominic Monaghan — what about a second fan club?

J.W. Braun — one of your favorite authors

Peter Jackson — director

Christopher Lee — "Saruman"

Dan Madsen — the fan club president

Citizens of Minas Tirith — it's there, I swear (under M)

Michael V. Regina — (xoanon) theonering.net cofounder

Brian Sibley — adapted *Lord of the Rings* to radio for the BBC

UofCSSDLBC Techies — The University of Chicago, Social Sciences Division Local Business Center Techies

Tom Underhill — we all know Mr. Underhill's *real* name

Elijah Wood — the first member of the fan club

Sonny Zwierkowski — has to wait a long time to see his name!

After Aragorn kills Lurtz, as he runs to the dying Boromir, one of the dead Orcs looks up to see what's going on.

As Boromir shares a last conversation with Aragorn, he grips Aragorn's shoulder from one angle. From the other angle, he doesn't.

Elijah Wood said he joined the fan club because he wanted to be sure his name was included in the credits. (Henny Garfunkel/ Retna/ Keystone Press)

The Fellowship of the Ring Easter Egg Alert

There is another Easter egg on the second disc of *The Fellowship of the Ring* Platinum Series Special Extended Edition. It's a preview of *The Two Towers* that followed some showings of *The Fellowship of the Ring* in April 2002. To access it, go to the "Select a Scene" menu and navigate to the final group of scenes. Then navigate down from Scene 48 to reveal a hidden "Two Towers" icon, and press "Enter."

Q&A
with Makeup Artist Vance Hartwell

Vance Hartwell, born in California, has spent decades working behind the scenes for commercials, television shows, and films. Being at the right place (Weta Workshop) at the right time, Hartwell joined *The Lord of the Rings* project right at its beginning. On July 15, 2002, fresh off the first film's success, he answered a few questions for me.

Braun: How did you become part of the film industry?
Hartwell: I was a film major in college. I had always wanted to make movies. Makeup just ended up being the first way "in" to the movies. Once I started working I really learned stuff. I'd say 99.9 percent of what I know I learned on the job.

Braun: What's it like living in New Zealand?
Hartwell: It took about a year to get used to living here. Coming from LA, it was like moving to the farm for us (me and my wife). We didn't think there'd be any culture shock since it was an English-speaking country. Well, there was. The shops closed up around 5 p.m. every weeknight and only a few things were open on Saturdays and then only for a couple of hours. Nothing, except petrol [gas] stations and dairies were open on Sundays. People here are more reserved and quieter than most Americans too. So there was some getting used to each other that took a while.

Braun: How did you become involved with *The Lord of the Rings*?
Hartwell: Well, I'd been working with Weta since 1993. My first project with them were the five Hercules telemovies. We worked on the Hercules series, the Xena series, did some New Zealand films and commercials, and some other things. Peter and Richard Taylor were/are partners in Weta, and so we just always did Peter's stuff when it came up.

When Peter told us he was going to make *The Hobbit*, I was pretty excited. When he told us that he wasn't going to do *The Hobbit*, but do *The Lord of the*

Rings, I was quite happy. It's a more difficult story to tell, but it had so much more potential. I first read the Lord of the Rings books when I was twelve. I fell in love with them. I think I read all three in a two-week period. I remember thinking, even then, that they would make great films. When the Bakshi film came out I forced my parents to take me to see it. They were bored stiff, but I loved it. I remember when we were in turnaround with Miramax on the project that I told Richard that even though the future of the project was uncertain that I was glad Peter was trying to get [another] studio to pick it up and let him do it right. It was a tough time for the shop as we didn't know if this job would happen and if it didn't, what our next job would be. It turned out alright though.

Braun: Tell us about what you did on the project.
Hartwell: Over the course of the project, I was involved in most areas of the creature and makeup effects. I was on from the beginning (early 1997) through the end of principal photography (December 2000). I made tons of molds, ran lots of foam latex, painted thousands of items, did some hair work, applied makeup onto the actors, puppeteered, and some stuff I can't even remember now.

Braun: You also designed the paint scheme for the Moria Orcs. What's special about this race?
Hartwell: Originally they were supposed to have very large eyes, since they live underground. The CG guys were going to enlarge all their eyes digitally. They did some tests that were pretty good, but the decision was made to "can" the idea as it would be very time consuming which in digital terms is very expensive. That's why the Goblins have a dark color around their eyes. It was the area where the eyes would enlarge and we would fill it in. You can see the enlarged eye effect in one of the shots.

Braun: What kind of contact lenses were used?
Hartwell: There were two types of lenses for the creatures: soft scleral and hard scleral. A scleral lens covers more than just the iris, it covers the white of the eye, too, called the sclera. I painted all of the hard scleral lenses for the Orcs, Uruk-hai and Goblins. Those lenses were only used in close-up shots though, as they were not optically pure. In other words, it was like looking through Vaseline.

Braun: Oh, so that's why the Orcs were always such lousy shots. It was because of your crummy contact lenses!
Hartwell: Apparently, there's only one or two companies in the world that still make

optically pure hard scleral lenses. They're rarely used anymore, what with the advances in soft contact lenses. Hard lenses gave us the ability to put in a lot of detail though.

The soft scleral lenses were painted by a company in Australia. They didn't have the detail of the hard ones and were used in more distant shots or where good vision was required, like fight scenes.

Frodo's "sick" eye [worn after the Nazgûl stabs him] was designed by Weta and made by a company in England. It was a soft scleral lens, but they did an amazing job of painting it.

Braun: There's been a lot of talk about the Hobbit feet being a pain to deal with.

Hartwell: I think a lot of what people are hearing is stuff just repeated and exaggerated in the retelling. All four guys were pretty happy with the feet. It was a pain having to wear them because they had to be careful with them when they weren't shooting. And, at the end of the day, they had to spend about a half hour having them removed and having their (real) feet cleaned when all they wanted to do was go home and sleep. There were some problems that popped up now and then, and we did our best to make whatever changes were needed so the feet would be as comfortable as possible for them all.

Braun: The ears worked well?

Hartwell: They were pretty simple items, just slip cast latex.

Braun: What did you think of the first film?

Hartwell: I enjoyed it. The hard thing though is that when I see it I remember all the other stuff that went on. It usually takes a few years before those memories fade and I can see a film I worked on as other people see it. Also, it was great seeing my daughter on-screen. She plays a Hobbit child in the birthday party scene at the beginning of the film.

Braun: Do you think Peter Jackson will ever make *The Hobbit?*

Hartwell: I don't know. It'd be nice if he did, but I also think it'd be kind of like going over the same ground again. I think he'll be wanting to do something different. Of course, if he does do it I'd like to work on it.

Braun: You've worked on many different projects. How was *The Lord of the Rings* special?

Hartwell: Well, I've never been on one project for four years before! That alone makes it stand out. Plus, the sheer number of items that were made. Over one of the Christmas breaks, I, along with another guy, painted over 100 Uruk-hai suits that had to be ready to go as soon as the crew came back from their holiday. It was hectic at times, but overall it was fun.

The Burden Is Heavy
Tolkien Wrote for One Audience;
The Scriptwriters Wrote for Four

Writing an original story has many advantages over adapting one — especially a popular one. Original scripts allow for more creativity, allow the writer to focus on what he or she wants to, and don't burden the writer with plot points that absolutely must be covered. The greatest advantage, however, is that the writer of an original story has only one audience to think about.

The writers who adapted *The Lord of the Rings* for the big screen didn't have this advantage. They were well aware that four distinct groups would be seeing these films, and it was important that every person who bought a ticket would get his or her money's worth. Who were these four audiences?

Those who read the books once or long ago:

The Lord of the Rings was huge in the 1960s, but then the mania died down. Add to this that the books were approaching an age of fifty years at the turn of the century, and you can understand why many people had last read the books long ago when seeing the films the first time. (When Jackson himself began working on the trilogy he hadn't read the books since the 1970s!)

The writers wanted to include the little moments which people tend to remember, even years after reading the books, such as the Nazgûl hunting the Hobbits in the wild, Sam cooking rabbits, and Pippin arriving at Minas Tirith. This way even a person who vaguely recalled the books could feel nostalgic while watching the films.

John Howe and Alan Lee, the Middle-earth equivalents to Van Gogh and da Vinci. (Ian Smith)

The fans who knew the books forward and backward:
These people didn't just know the books, they had studied them like they were handed down by the Creator. They were the geeks in the theater (like me) who noticed that Boromir's hair is wrong.

The scriptwriters inserted some inside jokes for these fans incorporating some of the chapter titles from *The Hobbit* and *The Lord of the Rings* into the dialogue ("Riddles in the Dark," "Not at Home," "A Shortcut to Mushrooms.") Also, by having the cinematography of the films mirror paintings by John Howe, Alan Lee, and Ted Nasmith, the filmmakers played to this group, who already knew these paintings as well as the rest of the world knows *The Starry Night* and *Mona Lisa*. The chapter titles and the replicas of the paintings went completely over the heads of those who weren't fanatics; thus, the writers were able to throw a wink at the serious fans without confusing everyone else.

Those who read *The Hobbit* but didn't start or finish *The Lord of the Rings*:

Before the films, I can't tell you how many times I heard, "Oh, Tolkien. He wrote *The Hobbit*, didn't he? I enjoyed it. I didn't really go much beyond that though." The truth is many readers either didn't start *The Lord of the Rings* because of its length, or gave up when they found out it isn't about Bilbo and it is nothing like *The Hobbit*.

The scriptwriters took care of this massive group of people by giving them a healthy dose of Bilbo and Gandalf early, and referencing *The Hobbit* numerous times. In fact, *The Fellowship of the Ring* sets up a prequel or two rather nicely. . . .

Those who didn't know Tolkien from Tolstoy:

It was paramount that these films carry their own weight, not needing the book to explain a character, a location, a motivation, or a story element to the viewers. The filmmakers didn't want this to be a film series just for readers; they wanted everyone to enjoy the adventure.

If it wasn't necessary for viewers to know a name or a place, such as Gil-galad or Lurtz, it wasn't mentioned. With the theatrical cuts, special care was taken to avoid confusing a virgin audience. Numerous story elements were left out (for example, Isildur doesn't put the Ring on, so the audience doesn't have to wonder why he disappears). The writers even wanted the people who would only see each film once to be able to follow and enjoy the entire trilogy.

While it would seem nearly impossible to cater to each of these groups without sacrificing the quality of the films as a whole, that the films appealed universally to everyone was an amazing feat, and a credit to the filmmakers.

THE LORD OF THE RINGS

The Two Towers

(2002)

(Jacquie Roland)

Directed by: Peter Jackson

Starring:

Elijah Wood as Frodo

Sean Astin as Sam

Andy Serkis as Gollum

Ian McKellen as Gandalf

Viggo Mortensen as Aragorn

Theatrical Cut: 2 hours 59 minutes   Bernard Hill as Théoden

Rated PG-13   Karl Urban as Éomer

Released December 18, 2002   Miranda Otto as Éowyn

Brad Dourif as Gríma Wormtongue

Extended Cut: 3 hours 43 minutes   Orlando Bloom as Legolas

Rated PG -13   John Rhys-Davies as Gimli

Released November 19, 2003   Christopher Lee as Saruman

David Wenham as Faramir

Domestic Gross: $341,786,758   Billy Boyd as Pippin

Worldwide Gross: $926,287,400   Dominic Monaghan as Merry

At first glance it seems ridiculous that *The Two Towers* book was adapted into its own film. It has no beginning. It has no ending. The characters are all scattered, participating in unrelated plots. One of the main battles is a group of talking trees versus a stone circle. One of the main characters is not just a member of a fictional species, but a deformed member of such. And yet it's not just a film, but a great one, with a central theme of keeping hope in a world of despair.

The Two Towers follows the remains of the broken Fellowship as they meet new adversaries and new friends. After the first film's "road" story, with its hidden Dwarvish realms and ethereal Elvish lands, the second film shifts gears. Our heroes enter the realms of Men, the relentless moving forward stops, and the focus of the story shifts from "the quest" to "defending the kingdom." While some may prefer the first film because its "quest" story continually introduces new realms, the advantage of the second film's story is that we finally get to pause and learn about the people and issues of one place, and witness the climactic battle that decides their fate.

And yet *The Two Towers* has always been the greatest obstacle for screenwriters attempting to adapt *The Lord of the Rings*. *The Fellowship of the Ring*, with the leads together participating in a linear plot, and *The Return of the King*, with the quest to destroy the Ring coming back into focus, lend themselves well to the cinema. Meanwhile, the middle child has an assorted group of headaches ready to take down the boldest of filmmakers. Jackson did not overcome all these challenges. The film starts off slowly because none of the characters is particularly well positioned to punch the plot forward. The theatrical cut is missing some vital scenes, because the story of the second film was more difficult to edit down to three hours than the more simplistic story of the first film. But these are minor issues. Overall, Jackson delivered a film that not only is entertaining in its own right, but does the dirty work that pays off the first film and sets up the third.

Will *The Two Towers*, that ridiculous idea that turned into such a great film, ever get the respect of its brothers? Perhaps not. It is, however, the lynchpin that holds the trilogy together.

Emyn Muil

Frodo has a dream about Gandalf before meeting Gollum and accepting him as a guide.

Emyn Muil, the impassable labyrinth of razor-sharp rocks.
(Tom Wuellette)

What the Big Folk Were Saying

"They're still barefoot."
— A mom as the film begins

"That guy must have lost a lot of weight for his part."
— A viewer who was unaware that Gollum is computer generated

"Someone tell that thing his comb-over isn't working."
— A man, talking about Gollum

What the Wizards Know

During production, the films were internally referred to as "Film One, Film Two, and Film Three."

The opening *"Lord of the Rings"* title shot was simply borrowed from the first film.

Gollum's musical theme is played on a cimbalom, a Hungarian hammered dulcimer that has a quivering uneasy feel. Howard Shore thought this instrument, which can be heard in the Shire music in The Fellowship of the Ring, *was quite appropriate to use for Gollum, a creature that was, after all, once a hobbit.*
(Rob Wiltbank)

Some of New Zealand's mountains are considered sacred, and the local tribes (which traditionally do not look at or photograph the peaks) were concerned about having the tops of these mountains in three blockbuster films. The filmmakers, therefore, agreed to replace these peaks with their own digital creations.

Gollum was the most difficult character in the trilogy to bring to life. Andy Serkis (Gollum) had to shoot each scene three times. First, he performed with the other actors in a Lycra bodysuit designed to make him as small as possible. Then the scene was shot again with him offstage giving his lines. Lastly, Serkis performed his part in a studio wearing a special suit that, with the use of computer software, captured his motions. The digital animators used this as a reference to create a computer-generated Gollum, placed either into the scene shot without Serkis, or the scene shot with him, but where he was painted out. Then, as the 200 animators worked on the subtleties of Gollum's performance, Serkis visited with them at their computers and offered suggestions. Even when the animators were finished, Serkis still had work to do: he had to voice Gollum once again — this time in a recording studio. In the end, the character was a true collaboration, driven by Serkis, involving hundreds of people.

While most filmgoers were annoyed with *Star Wars'* Jar Jar Binks, *Lord of the Rings* fans are fortunate he was created. According to Weta Digital, the breakthroughs in Binks' development were critical to the creation process of Gollum, a lead character chosen to be computer generated before *Star Wars: The Phantom Menace* (1999) proved it could be done.

What the Elvish Eyes and Ears Have Noticed

In the writer's commentary track for *The Two Towers*, Jackson mentions *Back to the Future Part II* (1989) noting how the two films open with a similar storytelling device. In the commentary track for *Back to the Future Part II*, writer Bob Gale mentions *The Lord of the Rings* films as Elijah Wood makes a brief appearance. (This DVD was released the same week as *The Two Towers*.)

The dialogue at the Bridge of Khazad-dûm has been edited slightly differently from the first appearance in *The Fellowship of the Ring*. Most notably, in *The Two Towers* Frodo screams before Gandalf loses his grip, as opposed to the prequel where he screams after.

The opening sequence of *The Two Towers* is not only great fun, but true to Tolkien's style of writing. Frodo's dream of Gandalf's fall and battle with the Balrog is an original idea of the films' writers, but dreams and visions play a similar role in the books.

There are whip scars on Gollum's back, reminding us of his stay in Mordor.

The Land of Rohan

Aragorn, Gimli, and Legolas pursue the Orcs, who have captured Merry and Pippin, while Saruman plots against Rohan. Learning that the Riders of Rohan have slaughtered the Orcs, Aragorn looks for signs of Merry and Pippin.

Rohan, home of the Horse-lords. (Heather Cuthull)

What the Big Folk Were Saying

"Hello? What? You have to call me back later, girlfriend, I'm watching *The Lord of the Rings!*"
— A woman on her cell phone

"Not hard to spot the bad guys, is it?"
— A boy to his father when Gríma Wormtongue appears

"Oh, I was waiting for the punchline."
— A woman, after Éomer asks what business an Elf, a Dwarf, and a Man have in the Riddermark

What the Wizards Know

The Plains of Rohan were Jackson's favorite location in the trilogy.

In the book, as the Uruk-hai take Merry and Pippin toward Isengard they are joined by Orcs (including Grishnákh) from Mordor. So when new Orcs arrive at this spot in the story in the extended edition, it's tempting to think they are from Mordor, and they are talking about Sauron growing impatient. This was not the film's intent, however. These Orcs have been sent (in a deleted scene) by Saruman to find out what's going on.

The helicopter shots of Aragorn, Legolas, and Gimli chasing after the Orcs were shot just after Mortensen had broken his toe, Bloom had broken a rib, and scale double Brett Beattie (Gimli) had dislocated his knee. (Pain is temporary. Film is forever.)

The Two Towers was created as an ambiguous title, but works for the book because of its two-part structure. The film, however, doesn't follow this structure, so the scriptwriters had to find another meaning. They certainly left no room for ambiguity: Orthanc and Barad-dûr were identified as the two towers by Gandalf in the first preview, and by Galadriel in the first teaser trailer. In the film, the same towers are specified as the "two" by Saruman.

Barad-dûr was the tallest miniature, standing about nine meters tall.

Rohan was designed to look like a kingdom from around 900 A.D.

Originally, the people of Rohan were going to have Irish accents, and filming began with this direction. The filmmakers changed their minds, however, and the Irish sounding lines were rerecorded in postproduction.

Alison Doody, famous for playing Dr. Elsa Schneider in *Indiana Jones and the Last Crusade* (1989), was asked to play Éowyn but declined because she wanted to spend time with her new daughter.

Kate Winslet, whose film career was launched by Jackson's *Heavenly Creatures* (1994), was offered the role of Éowyn, but declined as well.

Miranda Otto (Éowyn) was first shot with golden red hair, twisted back in a Pre-Raphaelite style. She was reshot with blond locks that usually fly free.

On the borders of Fangorn, Pippin asks Merry what's making a noise. Had Pippin asked the sound mixers he would have learned it's the pitched-down voice of a cow.

Most of the dialogue in these films had to be rerecorded in a studio because of background noise on set. When an actor only had a line or two, somebody who was already needed in the recording studio would often do his part. Serkis (Gollum) and Craig Parker (Haldir) both proved talented at creating voices. Serkis, in addition to voicing a Nazgûl in the first film, voiced three Orcs arguing about food at the edge of Fangorn Forest.

These dialogue sessions were conducted by writers Walsh and Philippa Boyens. With the actors concentrating more on dialogue than action, many of the lines were rerecorded in a more dramatic way than they had been originally spoken.

The actors who played the Riders of Rohan might surprise you. They were the same riders who played the Nazgûl: mostly women!

As filming progressed, the horses began picking up the terminology of the crew. When they heard "cameras rolling" or "action," they knew something was going to happen.

When Legolas believes Merry and Pippin have died, he says a line in Elvish that translates to "May they find peace in death." This was going to be subtitled, but the single line of text intruded on the moment and was dropped.

Upon kicking the Orc helmet, Aragorn's cry of frustration is a powerful moment. In truth, Mortensen cried out because he had just broken his toe.

What the Elvish Eyes and Ears Have Noticed

Jackson and Bakshi took two different approaches to using the character of Saruman. Tolkien doesn't give this wizard much mention in *The Fellowship of the Ring*, and Bakshi followed his lead, pushing his film toward confusion in the latter stages. In *The Two Towers* book the Rohan/Fangorn/Isengard plot pops up out of nowhere, forcing the audience to step aside from the main quest until its resolution — after which we can return to worrying about Sauron and the Ring for the remainder of the story. This sort of plot detour (a result of Tolkien not mapping out the story, but just making it up as he went along) is maddening for a filmmaker trying to adapt a book.

Jackson and his cowriters did not repeat Bakshi's mistake. They recognized the need to establish Saruman as a key villain early and did not wait, as the book does. We see him transform Isengard into ruin, burn the forest, breed Orcs, and send his Uruk-hai to capture the Hobbits as it happens, rather than finding out after the fact. And then there's one last master stroke: unlike the books, Saruman is presented in the films as Sauron's

Bakshi, in 1978, working on his adaptation of The Lord of the Rings. (Victoria Bakshi Yudis)

puppet. Thus, with a corporeal creature to speak for him, the films are able to keep Sauron an abstract flaming Eye while at the same time allowing him to be active in the films, even when the story focuses on Saruman and Rohan. These underappreciated changes have the audience prepared for *The Two Towers* before the film ever begins.

In the theatrical trailer, Aragorn tells Éomer, "We track a band of Uruk-hai." In the film, Aragorn says, "We track a party of Uruk-hai." You know the writers worked hard on these scripts when they debated between "band" and "party."

The Foolishness of a Took

Just as Uglúk stops the Uruk-hai the first time, one of them (just to the right of Uglúk's hand) falls to the ground.

Legolas says the Uruks are turning northeast and taking the Hobbits to Isengard. He might want to invest in a compass. The Uruks are turning northwest.

When Miramax was trying to condense the project into one film, the studio suggested that Gondor and Rohan be merged into one kingdom, with Éowyn and Boromir as brother and sister. (Someone check on Faramir. I think he just passed out.)

In the last two daytime shots of the Orcs (including one from the air), Merry and Pippin are absent.

Have the Orcs seen many menus?

In Éomer's first encounter with Aragorn, Gimli, and Legolas, just after Éomer takes his helmet off, there's a wide shot where he is talking, but no words are heard.

How does Aragorn know the Uruk-hai name? Has he been checking out TheOneRing.net on his BlackBerry?

Creating the Colors of Middle-earth
From the Green Dragon to the Grey Havens

The photographing of *The Lord of the Rings* took place over a period of four years, with some shots filmed when it was bright and sunny, and others when it was cloudy and grey. Some scenes included parts that were shot outdoors mixed with parts shot indoors. Other scenes included models and digital images. How was all this footage put together cohesively, allowing the viewer to focus on the story and not the weather?

Peter Doyle introduced new software for this trilogy, which allowed the filmmakers to color-correct and tone each piece of footage. In addition to allowing the filmmakers to match differently filmed shots for a scene, this new tool offered great freedom in shaping the look and feel of Middle-earth. For example, by manipulating the colors of a Rivendell, shifting them into a part of the palette nature doesn't really give us, the result subliminally creates a place that seems familiar but feels new. The filmmakers also learned how to manipulate the lighting, fading a scene to a darker color, echoing the emotion on-screen, over such a period of time that the audience doesn't realize it's happening, although it's felt subconsciously. The software was so advanced, the filmmakers could manipulate portions of each frame individually, enabling, for example, the color of the sky to be brightened as a scene progresses to reflect a mood, or to subtly whiten a character's face as he dies.

Perhaps most important, software allowed all the films to be shot simultaneously while still achieving Jackson's wish that each film would have its own individual look and feel, breaking up the monotony three identical films would have created.

Just before Éomer rides off, his sword falls out of its scabbard. I hope he discovers this before Helm's Deep. How embarrassing it would be if he were to appear at Gandalf's side saying, "Not alone," only to reach for his sword and find it missing.

Curiously, as Aragorn, Gimli, and Legolas examine the burning pile of Orc carcasses, they wear their Elvish brooches backward. Aragorn wears his scabbard on the reverse side. Legolas wears his quiver on the opposite shoulder. Aragorn also wears his Ring of Barahir on his right hand. It's like the entire scene has been flipped to get Fangorn Forest in the right place.

Fangorn Forest, the Dead Marshes, and the White Rider

Merry and Pippin flee into Fangorn Forest and encounter Treebeard. Meanwhile, Gollum leads Frodo and Sam into the Dead Marshes. Aragorn, Legolas, and Gimli unexpectedly find Gandalf, who asks them to come with him to Edoras.

The edge of Fangorn Forest was shot on location. The interior was shot in a studio. (Heather Cuthill)

What the Big Folk Were Saying

"That's Tall Paul, right?"

— A fan assuming scale double Tall Paul Randall was inside Treebeard's costume

"I see dead people."

— A young man when Frodo, Gollum, and Sam journey through the Marshes

"It's a Western."

— A woman when Gandalf, Legolas, Gimli, and Aragorn ride off on their horses

Rhys-Davies enjoyed voicing Treebeard, because the part required no makeup. (Chris Nielson)

What the Wizards Know

The filmmakers tried to locate a twisty, knurly forest for Fangorn, but they couldn't find one in New Zealand with the right look. In the end, they created its interior in a studio. An advantage to this was that the set (down to the leaves) could be scaled up — giving us less of the scale doubles and more of Monaghan and Boyd as Merry and Pippin.

Tolkien created Treebeard and the Ents because his son Michael asked him to make up a tale where a forest seeks revenge for being wronged.

Jackson worried that his design team would have trouble creating Ents that could be viewed as serious actors as opposed to cartoon characters. When design artist Daniel Falconer presented Jackson with his first drawing of Treebeard, Jackson couldn't believe how perfect it was. The design of Ents followed this lead.

Rhys-Davies not only played Gimli, he was also the voice of Treebeard.

While preparing to shoot the Beacons of Minas Tirith from a helicopter, the filmmakers saw an interesting marshland. They shot this as well and used it for the overhead shot of the Dead Marshes.

The close-ups of the Dead Marshes were shot in an artificial set built in the same place as the Doors of Moria.

The dead bodies in the Marshes are the fallen warriors from the battle that opens the first film. Theoretically, there should be dead Orc bodies in the Marshes as well. (Gollum even says as much.) Jackson did not want them included because he thought they might confuse viewers who didn't understand they were dead.

As Gollum beckons the Hobbits into the Marshes, the shot matches *Through the Marshes*, a painting by Ted Nasmith for the 1996 Tolkien Calendar.

The opening shot of *The Return of the King*, exploring how Sméagol became Gollum, was originally going to follow the part in *The Two Towers* where Frodo talks to Gollum about Gollum's past. It even begins with a moment meant to parallel Gollum holding a worm just before Frodo tosses him some *lembas* bread (in the extended edition only). As originally conceived, the flashback was to start right after Gollum speaks his real name, Sméagol, for the first time in centuries and then end with the scream of the Nazgûl taking us back to the present. (Look at that — Peter Jackson almost invented the TV show *Lost*.) However, the sequence slowed the theatrical cut of *The Two Towers* down, so the Ring-finding/Gollum-transforming bit was set aside for the extended edition. By the time that project was in the works, Jackson thought it might be a fun opening to the next film.

Blanco, standing by in case Demero causes any trouble.

(Philippa Ballantine)

For Shadowfax's glorious entrance into the film, Demero (Shadowfax), when called, was trained to approach a board near which McKellen was standing. But, just in case Demero didn't cooperate, another horse, Blanco, was trained to do the same. As it turned out, Demero did Shadowfax's glorious entrance in one take.

Because the lead horses were needed for so long, the filmmakers bought them rather than rented them. When shooting was completed, the horses were auctioned off. (Some of them were bought by members of the cast or crew.)

What the Elvish Eyes and Ears Have Noticed

Treebeard talks and acts like the Rockbiter from *The NeverEnding Story* (1984), a film that mentions *The Lord of the Rings*, incidentally.

Actors in a film are lit with multiple lights. An actor's eyes, an important tool, are given a special light of their own. Gollum, of course, is computer generated and not lit on set at all. However, if you look closely, you'll see his eyes appear to be lit with an eyelight just like the other characters, giving off the same small highlight.

Considering their material and design, Gandalf's new cloak and staff are clearly gifts from the Lady Galadriel. (According to Tolkien, Gandalf arrived in Lothlórien the day after the Fellowship departed. Imagine if Frodo had just stayed a little longer.)

Notice who no longer has a hat.

Gandalf wasn't the only one to lose his hat. The filmmakers did too! After the completion of principal photography in 2000, the hat was loaned to a Los Angeles costume exhibition for a few weeks. When it was shipped back to New Zealand it was lost in the mail. In 2003 it was discovered at an Air New Zealand "lost property" auction in Wellington. I wonder how much it would have sold for?

Legolas rarely blinks. But when Shadowfax appears, he blinks several times.

As Gandalf, Aragorn, Legolas, and Gimli ride toward Edoras, villages burn in the distance.

Having Treebeard take Merry and Pippin to the White Wizard was a clever invention of the scriptwriters. It not only makes Treebeard's introduction more dramatic and doubles the joy of discovering the White Wizard to be Gandalf, it saves the next film the hassle of introducing Gandalf the White to Merry and Pippin at Isengard.

That clever Howard Shore snuck an important musical theme into the extended edition of *The Two Towers*. As Gandalf speaks to Aragorn in the night of Frodo and the Ring, "The Fate of the Ring" theme quietly plays in the background. The theme is not heard again until *The Return of the King*, where it plays a key role, including the scene as Barad-dûr crumbles before the eyes of the Men of the West.

The wise must have foreseen something that has led to a mistaken belief. Gandalf repeats Galadriel's hint that Frodo must complete his quest alone, and he seems genuinely surprised (though pleased) that Sam is with him. In fact, Gandalf and Galadriel are proven to be wrong in the next film, as it will take three to complete the quest.

The Foolishness of a Took

When Pippin climbs Treebeard, he has blood on his face, but the blood is gone shortly afterward. Apparently, even in his frightened state, Pippin wants to look his best.

The old Ent sure gets his wooden undies in a bundle when Pippin calls him a tree. Then he asks to be called Treebeard. Well, heck, just imagine how angry he would have been had Pippin called him something that *wasn't* half his name!

The Black Gate, Edoras, and the Wilderness

Frodo arrives at the Black Gate, but Gollum convinces him to try to enter Mordor another way. Gandalf and company arrive at Edoras and free King Théoden from Saruman's control. Théoden, learning that his realm is under attack, decides to lead his people away from its capital city. While Frodo and Sam sleep, Gollum has an internal debate that ends with him banishing his evil side. However, he is separated from Frodo and Sam when they are captured by Faramir.

The view of Rohan from Edoras, its capital city. (Heather Cuthill)

What the Big Folk Were Saying

"Wait, which one is Rick?"

— A woman after Éowyn says the wild men are burning rick, cot, and tree

"I knew it from the beginning! There are two of them creatures. I've noticed it. They're slightly different."

— A man upon seeing Gollum talk to Sméagol

What the Wizards Know

The Black Gate miniature was sculpted in lead.

The shot of Gollum and the Hobbits peering at the Black Gate was shot at a basketball court.

Astin was not having very much fun at this point in the shoot. The day before shooting the Black Gate stuff, he had cut his foot filming the ending of *The Fellowship of the Ring*, and the swollen, stitched result made it difficult for him to hobble around. Then, while filming the exciting moment when Sam and Frodo are about to dash into Mordor only to be stopped by Gollum, Serkis pulled Astin's wig off, forcing him to return to the hair and make-up bus before shooting could continue.

All the lead actors were wigged. Their real hair was slicked back with a gel that when dry had a texture similar to concrete. The wig was then glued onto the forehead and pinned in the back. Some of the actors, such as Orlando Bloom, cut their hair very short to aid the process.

Khamûl, the Nazgûl who nearly catches Frodo at the ferry, was once King of the Easterlings, the race Gollum and the Hobbits spy entering Mordor.

Because so many added scenes included Gollum and Treebeard — which meant a lot of visual effect shots — the extended edition of *The Two Towers* required much more work than the extended edition of *The Fellowship of the Ring*.

Edoras took eight months to build. Shooting took eight days.

Jackson thought Edoras might have to be shot with a combination of miniatures and visual effect shots, but his scouts found a location that matched Tolkien's detailed description of the place word for word. When the Art Department had finished their construction of the buildings, Jackson had as real an Edoras as Middle-earth could have provided. But this did create some challenges for the more practical aspects of filmmaking. Jackson was going to film 360 degrees from the highest point, and yet there had to be areas for trucks, offices, equipment, bathrooms, a first aid area, a place for lunch, and stabling for 200 horses. Fortunately, there were no real people of Rohan living there, so the houses were used for support facilities and storage, lunch was served at the Golden

Hall itself, and art director Dan Hennah created a large rock with a hidden corridor inside for the vehicles.

A ten-acre field of wheat was purchased and harvested exclusively to construct the roofs.

The location was so windy, the structures had to be built deep into the ground to remain standing. The thatched roofs had to be covered with nets (invisible to the camera) to keep the wheat in place. Some of the actors (including McKellen) even had to have beards and capes sewed onto their costumes to keep them in place.

The heavy double-barred doors of the Golden Hall were built with a complex locking system that involved two sliding, pivoting beams that could be lowered and secured in place. The locking system did not end up being used in the film.

Alan Lee's daughter created Théoden's wooden throne.

Instant potato flakes were used for Wormtongue's dandruff.

"Éowyn's Lament," which Miranda Otto sings in the extended edition at Théodred's funeral, was written by the film's linguist David Salo and composed by Plan 9. Its Rohirric lyrics translate to: "An evil death has sent forth the noble warrior. A song shall sing sorrowing minstrels Meduseld, that he was of men dearest to his lord and bravest of kinsmen. An evil death. . . ."

The digital effects team had to add people to Théodred's funeral because not enough extras were available.

An elaborate sequence involving an Orc attack at night (which had the Orcs setting fire to Edoras) was dropped because of the difficulties of lighting Edoras after dark.

After the movies were released, Serkis received letters from fans who had battled addictions and had weight problems who identified with Gollum's internal struggle against self-hatred.

Bloom auditioned for the part of Faramir and seemed a perfect fit. However, Legolas proved more difficult to cast. After nearly giving up hope of finding the perfect Elf, Jackson thought about Bloom as Legolas, as Faramir would be easy to recast.

Ethan Hawke and Uma Thurman, married at the time, were asked if they would play Faramir and Éowyn. Hawke, a fan of the books, was interested, but Thurman decided to pass, and then Hawke did as well.

What the Elvish Eyes and Ears Have Noticed

In the extended edition, Merry and Pippin are swallowed up by a tree. This is one of several moments the writers borrowed from a different part of the corresponding story in the books.

Merry and Pippin don't actually change size as they do in the book. The same tricks and scale doubles were used throughout the trilogy of films. Thus, when they argue about size in the extended edition of this film we can conclude the issue is all in their heads, which fits the characters.

Would you believe the film's writers have given some of Gandalf's lines to . . . Wormtongue?! When Wormtongue talks to Éowyn of speaking to the darkness, the walls closing in, and a hutch to trammel some wild thing in, he's borrowing a speech by Gandalf from the written version of *The Return of the King*!

The Rohirric Gandalf speaks to say goodbye to Théodred translates to: "Be-thou well. Go-thou, Théodred, go-thou."

As Gandalf pleads with Théoden to fight, he places his hand on the king's throne. Théoden gives him a look, and Gandalf subtly moves his hand away. In the book, people are often questioning Gandalf's motives, believing his ambition is to gather power. This simple and subtle piece of acting explores this issue better than any dialogue ever could.

Bernard Hill was the perfect choice for Théoden. (Ian Smith)

Aragorn's Elvish at the stable in the extended edition translates to, "Easy, quiet now . . . easy. Quiet now . . . quiet . . . it's okay now. What is your name? Brego? Your name is kingly. What troubles you, Brego? What did you see?"

As Frodo and Sam argue about saving Gollum, the Amon Sûl ruins can be seen in the background. (Do you notice that these ruins seem to be following the Hobbits?)

With Gandalf and Aragorn elsewhere, the scriptwriters must have found it more difficult to write the scenes with the Hobbits. Without a character to explain new places and new situations in a story, the audience can quickly become confused. Fortunately, the writers were able to depend upon Treebeard and, believe it or not, Gollum, to fill this role.

The unique musical sound that represents the Rohan culture comes from a Norwegian Hardanger fiddle. This instrument is similar to a violin but has extra "resonance" strings that produce a haunting echo effect when the main strings are played. Shore learned of the instrument while researching sounds for The Two Towers *score and thought the fiddle perfectly represented Rohan's proud but sorrowful culture.* (Karen Myers)

The Foolishness of a Took

When Legolas is asked to turn over his weapons, he reaches behind his back for his knives and gives them up. Then, as Aragorn hands over his sword, we see Legolas reaching for his knives again.

As Gandalf approaches Théoden for the first time, his staff alternates between being upright and parallel with the floor.

Just to show us he's every bit the wizard Gandalf is, Saruman performs some magic of his own. When he orders Warg riders to be sent out, his staff is in his right hand. Then suddenly the staff is in his left hand.

After Saruman asks Sharku, the Orc captain to send the Warg riders, the captain moves his lips in reply, but no sound is heard.

The Two Towers Easter Egg Alert

There's a hidden bonus feature included with the *The Two Towers* Platinum Series Special Extended Edition (the four-disc set that comes in a red box). It is Gollum's 2003 MTV Movie Awards speech, and it is not suitable for children. To access it, go to the "Select a Scene" menu on the first disc and navigate to the final group of scenes. Then navigate down from Scene 30 to reveal a hidden Ring symbol and press "Enter."

Aragorn, Éowyn, and Arwen

On the way to the fortress of Helm's Deep, the people of Rohan, along with Aragorn, Legolas, and Gimli, are attacked by Orcs riding on Wargs. The evil creatures are defeated, but Aragorn is separated from the rest, who arrive safely at the fortress.

Arwen's magical jewel, the Evenstar, symbolizes her life and her heart. (Tom Wuellette)

What the Big Folk Were Saying

"Back off my man, woman!"
— A girl as Éowyn smiles at Aragorn

"They said there was no sex in this movie!"
— A mom (before walking out with her fifteen-year-old son) when Arwen appears in Aragorn's dream

What the Wizards Know

Dunedin, the second largest city on New Zealand's South Island, has a soccer team called the Dunedin Rangers. The crew would sometimes joke about Aragorn being on the team.

Both Snaga, the Orc who wants to eat Merry and Pippin, and Sharku, the Orc who steals Aragorn's Evenstar, were played by Jed Brophy. Brophy is one of New Zealand's best horseback riders. He also played a Rider of Rohan as well as one of the Nazgûl pursuing Arwen in the first film. He even saved Karl Urban (Éomer) when Urban was on a horse that suddenly decided to bolt.

Brophy had to wear such large teeth for Sharku, his words on set came out somewhat like, "Tha tha tha tha, da tha." He nearly had the crew rolling on the floor with laughter.

What the Elvish Eyes and Ears Have Noticed

Fans of the book can watch *The Fellowship of the Ring* for the first time and probably know (more or less) what's coming next. *The Two Towers*, however, strays from Tolkien's story and structure considerably and even a longtime fan is sure to be uncertain, upon a first viewing, of what the next scene will be. In the second half, Jackson's *Two Towers* abandons Tolkien's story almost altogether, with scene after scene of original ideas. As someone who has read the books many times, I find this fresh and exciting. It feels like I'm going to the same favorite place, but taking a different path. I also find it impressive that the second half of *The Two Towers*, which is more Jackson than Tolkien, fits in so well with the rest of the film trilogy — which is more Tolkien than Jackson. This shows us how well the scriptwriters understood Middle-earth.

Gimli's lines about the scarcity of Dwarf women come straight from *The Lord of the Rings* Appendix A.

When Aragorn has his "good dream" (that's an understatement) he's wearing no shoes, another reference to Appendix A, where Aragorn is described as walking "unshod" with Arwen.

The sequence of events regarding Aragorn's relationship with Arwen is shown out of chronological order, spread over theatrical and extended editions, and thus sometimes confuses viewers. Here is the sequence in its proper chronological order:

Liv Tyler performed Arwen with a grace and maturity befitting the Elf. (Lisa O'Connor/ Zuma Press/ Keystone Press)

- Arwen gives Aragorn the Evenstar jewel just before the Council of Elrond, as shown in the first film.
- The night before the Fellowship departs, Aragorn and Arwen share the romantic moment he later remembers in his "good dream" in *The Two Towers*. Arwen tells her boytoy that he must go with Frodo and trust in their love.
- The next day, as the Fellowship prepares to depart — and after a tongue lashing from Elrond — Aragorn tries to give the Evenstar back to Arwen. If you look carefully, you can see the other members of the Fellowship to the left as Aragorn walks toward his honey. But Arwen tells him to keep it. (This, too, is shown in *The Two Towers*.)
- Moments later, Elrond addresses the Fellowship (as seen in the extended edition of *The Fellowship of the Ring*) and Arwen gives Aragorn a last look, as if to say, "It will be okay."

The way Arwen closes Aragorn's hand around the Evenstar while asking him to keep it must be influential. Aragorn closes Frodo's hand around the Ring in the same way as they say goodbye at the end of the first film.

A few seconds of music from *The Fellowship of the Ring* were edited directly into *The Two Towers*. As Legolas sees the Wargs coming over the hill in the distance, music from the Moria staircase sequence plays.

The Warg attack is another example of the writers moving events around. In Tolkien's story it happens to the Fellowship in *The Fellowship of the Ring*.

If Legolas existed in the real world, his horse-mounting skills would make him a YouTube sensation. Interestingly, his spectacular way of mounting his horse came about by accident. Originally the filmmakers intended to shoot close-ups of Bloom's hands, feet, and body mounting a horse and tightly edit them together. Bloom, however, was injured falling off a horse (breaking a rib as mentioned earlier) and a wide shot of him reaching for the saddle was all they had to work with when shooting ended at the location. When pickup shots were done in 2002, Bloom wasn't available because he had grown facial hair for *Ned Kelly* (2003) and wasn't allowed to shave. So Jackson had to ask his visual effects team to take care of it. They painted out Bloom (who, after reaching for the saddle, simply let the horse run by) and digitally animated him flipping onto his horse.

After Aragorn falls over the cliff, the shot of Théoden, Legolas, and Gimli peering over is similar to a scene in *Indiana Jones and the Last Crusade* (1989). Rhys-Davies is not only in both scenes, he appears the same height because, coincidently, he happened to be on his knees looking over the cliff in *Indiana Jones!* (When I first saw *The Two Towers* and saw a figure approach the peerers from behind, I half-expected it to be Aragorn . . . or Indiana Jones. But it was Gamling.)

The road to Helm's Deep. (David Forbes)

Legolas has never had to deal with death before this adventure, so in these films he goes through all the stages of grief in succession. When Gandalf dies, he's confused. When Boromir dies, he looks on with pity. When he discovers the apparent death of the Hobbits, he's sad. When Aragorn appears to die, he gets very angry. This is like his own private twelve-step program.

The Foolishness of a Took
When everyone's looking for Aragorn, Sharku chuckles and says he's dead. Apparently Orcs are not only familiar with menus, they also know who Aragorn is.

A New Power Is Rising

Saruman sends his army to Helm's Deep. Aragorn is rescued by Brego the horse. Elrond convinces Arwen to depart Middle-earth while Galadriel ponders the future. Faramir takes Frodo and Sam to Henneth Annûn, a secret hideout, where he captures Gollum and learns of the Ring.

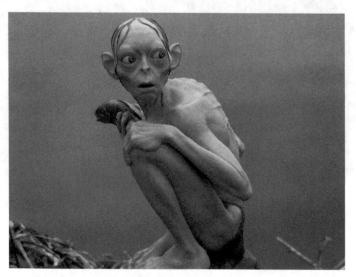

The Two Towers *Collector's Gift Set came with this polystone statue, depicting Gollum at the Forbidden Pool.* (J.W. Braun)

What the Big Folk Were Saying
"Holy . . . !"

— A group of teenagers when Isengard is revealed to be full of Orcs

What the Wizards Know
The Orcs' responses to Saruman at the "pep rally" were provided by 25,000 cricket fans at Westpac Stadium in Wellington, New Zealand. The fans screamed war chants spelled out on the Diamond Vision screen, with Peter Jackson himself leading the crowd.

In addition to auditioning for Denethor, John Noble auditioned for the part of Saruman.

Mortensen's scariest moment in the shoot came when he had to let the river carry him just prior to Aragorn's reawakening. The river's rapids were stronger than anticipated, the current caught him, and he was pulled under water some fifteen feet. After a frightening few moments, he was able to free himself and swim to the surface, where the crew quickly came to his aid.

Not only was Mortensen a last-minute replacement, his horse was too. Uraeus (Brego) had never been on a film set before and did a lot of learning throughout the project. As the shoot progressed, he began trusting in Mortensen more and more, and Mortensen considered Uraeus a member of the cast. The Ranger bought the horse after filming concluded.

Arwen's vision of Aragorn's death was written into the script after a fan wrote a letter to the scriptwriters about the passage in the appendices it was based on, mentioning that it was Tolkien's best writing.

For the departing Rivendell Elves, it was discovered that fifty Elven lamps were needed just two days before the scene was to be filmed. Nonetheless, the lamps were designed, constructed, and delivered on time. (It helped that they were only cardboard.)

An unused scene was filmed where Elrond, Galadriel, Celeborn, and Haldir discuss the current situation and agree to send an army to Helm's Deep.

Jackson has said that of all the characters Tolkien created, Faramir was the most difficult for him to deal with. He's a character that another scriptwriter would have been tempted to drop, as he's not important to the overall story. Frodo doesn't change his plans because of anything the young captain says or does, and Faramir is a minor character in *The Return of the King*. Jackson, however, knew book readers would be disappointed if he were not present and did his best to make him (and his part in the story) interesting.

In early drafts of the script, Denethor appeared at the Council of Elrond.

What the Elvish Eyes and Ears Have Noticed

The hardest part about making *The Two Towers* as a standalone film must have been figuring out how to deal with the intertwining chronology of the three books. For example, the last chapter of *The Two Towers* takes place on March 13 — after the first chapter of *The Return of the King* which happens on March 9. The second chapter of *The Return of the King* begins before either of these chapters — on March 6! Trying to sort this all out and create a film with good pacing would be difficult enough, but trying to separate the intertwining books into separate films seems a fool's errand. Yet the scriptwriters were able to do so. To accomplish this, some events from *The Two Towers* book, such as Boromir's death and Shelob's attack, appear in *The Fellowship of the Ring* and *The Return of the King* films. Also, some of the chronology has been altered. For example, in the books when Théoden arrives at Helm's Deep, Merry and Pippin have already been taken by the Ents to Isengard, and Frodo and Sam are between the Dead Marshes and the Black Gate. In the films, when Théoden arrives at Helm's Deep, Entmoot has not yet happened, and Frodo and Sam are with Faramir. That most people don't notice the work the scriptwriters did is a testament to how well they did it.

When Wormtongue sees the Orc army about to be unleashed upon Rohan, a single tear falls down his cheek. No doubt this is for Éowyn, whom he really does love. (Okay, so I just happen to be a Gríma/Éowyn shipper. Is that wrong? Don't answer that.)

In the vision of Aragorn's death, Elrond paints the picture as if Aragorn has become King. And sure enough, Aragorn's sword in the vision is not the one he carries in this (or the previous) film, but rather Andúril, the symbol of the Kingship.

The tapestry in Arwen's room shows the Two Trees of Valinor and a ship, the symbols of the undying lands. Elrond must have personally decorated her room.

As a great actor who looks like he could be Sean Bean's brother, David Wenham was a natural as Faramir. (Robert Millard/ Zuma Press/ Keystone Press)

Arwen calls Elrond "Ada," which the subtitle generously translates as "father." However, "Adar" is father. "Ada" is more along the lines of "daddy."

The Boromir/Faramir/Denethor scene, which appears in the extended edition, looks fabulous on the big screen, but sadly didn't make the theatrical cut. Filmed in 2002 as a pickup shot it's an interesting moment, as Boromir appears almost exclusively in its prequel, and Denethor appears almost exclusively in its sequel, yet here we see them with Faramir, a pivotal character in the middle film.

David Wenham (Faramir) and Sean Bean (Boromir) really do resemble one another in appearance. In particular, they have the same nose.

When Boromir says, "Life is good" in the extended edition and demands drink for his men, I can't help but wonder if I'm watching a beer commercial.

The Foolishness of a Took

Why is Wormtongue walking around Orthanc with a candle? He even takes it outside with him to view Saruman's army. Perhaps someone was watching *Army of Darkness* and thought it would be cute to repeat the scene where a simpleton uses a candle to view an explosive substance, only to have the wiser character catch his arm and push him away.

When Aragorn mounts Brego by the river, the horse has no saddle. However, when Aragorn sees the Orc army, Brego has one. (I suppose he could have found one along the way.)

Faramir needs to talk to his cartographer. His map has several spelling mistakes: "Black Gates," "Helms Deep," and "Dagorland." The map also omits Minas Morgul.

Merchandise Gone Wild

It fascinates me that not only were people paid to create these items linked to the movies, but that fans rushed out to buy them. Here is the "dark side" of *The Lord of the Rings* film phenomenon: the merchandising world, featuring some of the zaniest items that were actually marketed, sold, and collected. (I just know some people are going to use this as an actual shopping checklist.)

The Ringwraith Bank with Sound: Who needs a piggy bank when you can get one that will scream at you every time you insert a coin? For ages 6 and up!

The Burger King Toys: I don't know which was worse, the toys themselves, or the commercial where a group of kids, exploring "Middle-earth" stumbled across a Burger King as the narrator told us, *"Lord of the Rings* comes to Burger King with nineteen magical toys. . . . You can collect and trade them to build the awesome Ring of Power!" Thankfully the toys have been forgotten, and the commercials were off the air by the time the films became a phenomenon.

Never trust an Elf . . . you can buy at Burger King. (J.W. Braun)

Saruman's Candle Holder: They've taken the top of Saruman's staff and turned it into a candle holder; for your very own Orthanc.

Evil Doormats: Nothing says, "Welcome to my home" quite like an image of Mordor on your doormat. I wonder if Sauron has one at Barad-dûr?

***Lord of the Rings* Cereal:** Yes, courtesy of Nestlé's Cinnamon Grahams, you can enjoy your morning meal with Saruman leering at you from the box.

The Oversized Sméagol Talking Doll: Apart from looking like a deformed alien, this "highly poseable" plush toy speaks one of four phrases when squeezed. Another variation has switchable heads so you can choose what mood you wish him to be in. This is proof that there is a toymaker out there who delights in frightening children. (That said, one woman proved these things can have a practical purpose. She placed a life-size Sméagol doll in her passenger seat so she could use the carpool lane.)

The Lord of the Rings Pinball Machine: This game, "featuring exciting elements from all three films," was released in 2003. The goal is to collect the Great Rings of power from the various races, thereby creating the One Ring, which you must then destroy. See, it's just like the films!

The Lord of the Rings Epic Scale Balrog: It's not that it looks bad, it's just *really* big and *really* expensive. Are there really people willing to spend hundreds of dollars on a light-up figure with a forty-two-inch wingspan? (Don't answer that.)

Barbie and Ken as Arwen and Aragorn: Yes, thanks to Mattel, collectible Barbie and Ken bring the "sweeping splendor" of Middle-earth to your little one's room. The dolls are dressed up for the coronation. Being Queen and King was perhaps too much pressure, however. Mattel announced the couple's breakup less than two months after *The Return of the King* was released.

"I'm an Arwen-girl, in an Arwen-world. Life in plastic, it's fantastic!" (Amanda Mikeska)

The full Moon sets at Henneth Annûn as Faramir points out Gollum to Frodo. Tolkien's version of this scene takes place at dawn, but the filmmakers shifted it to an earlier time. Unfortunately (for the filmmakers) the full Moon always sets at dawn.

When Sam suggests to Frodo that they use the Ring to escape, Frodo says he can't. Meanwhile, the barrels next to them say they can. Before Faramir arrives, the barrels evidently put on their own Rings of Power and turn invisible.

Helm's Deep

Aragorn arrives at Helm's Deep and warns Théoden of Saruman's army, which soon arrives and lays siege. Treebeard takes Merry and Pippin to Entmoot, a gathering of the Ents, and Faramir takes Frodo to Osgiliath. While Gandalf saves the day at Helm's Deep, the Ents sack Isengard.

Helm Hammerhand, the ninth king of Rohan, greets visitors to his fortress. (Ben Watkin)

What the Big Folk Were Saying

"Middle-earth reminds me of high school."
— A young lady when Éowyn watches Legolas return the Evenstar to Aragorn

"Oh, my baby is back!"
— A teenage girl when Haldir appears

"Run, forest, run!"
— A man as the Ents decide to go to war

"The sound is out. Hey, someone tell the theater people we have a problem here! We've lost the sound!"
— Several people when Sam's voice fades out while talking to Frodo at Osgiliath

What the Wizards Know

Éowyn is another character that other scriptwriters might have eliminated. In the books, she does almost nothing in *The Two Towers*, and her subplot in *The Return of the King* begins at a time when most other subplots are drawing to a conclusion. The filmmakers, however, recognized how her character could enrich the films and gave her a larger role, developing her character earlier in the story than Tolkien did, and borrowing some of her lines from *The Return of the King* book for use in *The Two Towers* film.

A year and a half after Bruce Hopkins attended a generic Uruk-hai audition, he was asked to play Gamling, a rather undefined character at that point. As filming proceeded, Hopkins picked up a lot of lines, especially at Helm's Deep, as the writers discovered they needed someone to deliver Théoden's orders to the men.

King Théoden's breastplate has Rohirrim symbols engraved on the inside. Unseen by the camera, they were created to help Bernard Hill feel more in character.

The battle at Helm's Deep presented the greatest challenge to preserving continuity. It was not shot in script order, and it was important to know, for example, just how many arrows Legolas should have in his quiver for any particular shot so that when the final edit was put together his quiver would appear to slowly empty. Meanwhile, Gimli and Aragorn — as well as their weapons — needed more mud and blood as the fight progressed.

Most people know that blood in films is not real. But even some actors are surprised that the mud isn't either. Real mud is not sanitary and cannot be used. This film manufactured its own mud, which was stored in refrigerators with an expiration date.

Whenever a battle was being filmed in this trilogy, the cast and crew were sure to see the "gore" truck nearby, with its crew members ready to make the actors appear bloody and injured.

The casting department ran out of fair-skinned, blue-eyed extras to play the Rohan soldiers. Brown-skinned, brown-eyed Maori boys were placed in the background. They were nicknamed the "Bro-han."

They also ran out of tall men to play the Uruk-hai. The shorter Orcs were called the Uruk-low.

There are many styles of sword fighting. An axe can be used in battle in various ways as well. A bow, however, can be used in only one way: to shoot an arrow. This can quickly become boring to watch. For this reason, the filmmakers tried to be creative with Legolas, finding new ways for him to use his arrows, such as shooting while surfing down a staircase at Helm's Deep.

While battling at the gates of Helm's Deep, Hopkins sliced Hill's ear, causing the king to be taken away from Helm's Deep in an ambulance. It was just three days into filming for Hopkins, who took out the man 10,000 Orcs could not.

When a line in a film becomes a favorite with fans, it's not unusual for the line to be referenced in the sequel. What is unusual is for the sequel's reference to have been filmed not only before the first film was even released, but before the referenced line itself was shot: Gimli's "Toss me!" was filmed before "Nobody tosses a Dwarf."

Footage was shot of Éowyn delivering Morwen's baby in the Glittering Caves, giving Éothain and Freda a new sibling.

Osgiliath used pieces from so many other sets, some of the crew thought of it as "Middle-earth's greatest hits."

The Orcs may not like Bernard Hill or Viggo Mortensen, but the fans sure do! (Seth Daire)

So what does Sam say when the sound fades out? "Hold on, Mr. Frodo, you'll be alright. Don't worry. We'll get through this. Just as we've always done."

The horses at Helm's Deep are theoretically kept in an underground stable that connects to the Keep. Conceived by the Art Department, the filmmakers never got around to actually building this set, so the audience is left to imagine it. (There's one for you fan artists.)

To avoid slipping, the horses exiting the fortress of Helm's Deep had to wear rubber shoes and run along a surface painted with a special epoxy paint.

What the Elvish Eyes and Ears Have Noticed

Just as described in the book, some of the stonework at Helm's Deep looks to have been recently and hastily repaired.

When Théoden facetiously asks Aragorn whether Elves or Dwarves will come, there's an extra behind him playing patty-cake with a toddler to entertain the child.

Elijah Wood's sister, Hannah, gets a close-up. She's the blond, lost-looking girl entering the Glittering Caves.

The hair restoration industry should thank Eru they don't live in Rohan.

When Legolas lashes out about the hopelessness of the fight, conceptual artist Alan Lee and art director Dan Hennah can be seen to the left of Aragorn as the men of Rohan.

In commercials that aired in December 2002, Aragorn says, "These are my people, and I shall die as one of them!" The first part, "these are my people," must have been cut just before the film hit the theaters. Perhaps people were confused at test screenings, wondering if Aragorn is from Rohan.

Writer Philippa Boyens' son Calem played Haleth, son of Háma, while Mortensen's son Henry played the boy to his right just before Mortensen says, "Give me your sword."

In the film *Distant Drums* (1951), a character eaten by an alligator lets out a scream (which was actually performed by a voice actor in a recording studio after the scene was filmed). Since then, as an inside joke, the Wilhelm scream, as it is now known, has been edited into well over 100 films, including *The Charge at Feather River* (1953), *The Green Berets* (1968), *Star Wars* (1977), *Beauty and the Beast* (1991), *Spider-Man* (2002), *Pirates of the Caribbean: The Curse of the Black Pearl* (2003), and *Transformers* (2007). Jackson was unaware of the joke when *The Fellowship of the Ring* was made, but was told of its history while *The Two Towers* was in post-production. He not only wanted it included, he asked for it to be extra loud. Listen for it soon after the ladders are raised when an Elf plunges to his death.

Jackson's and Walsh's children appear again, this time as Rohirrim children hiding in the caves.

Jackson, himself, has another cameo as a spear-throwing Man of Rohan.

When Haldir dies, the musical theme that plays is the same as when Aragorn looks upon his mother's grave in the *The Fellowship of the Ring* extended edition.

Treebeard wants to take Merry and Pippin to the western borders of Fangorn. Pippin responds that it would be better if Treebeard took them south. Pippin's right. If they go west, they'll hit the mountains. If they go south, they can take the Gap of Rohan and follow safe paths to the Shire . . . assuming they make it past Saruman.

The Amon Sûl ruins continue to follow Frodo and Sam, appearing again at Osgiliath.

The Foolishness of a Took
Théoden really must find better scouts. It's a time of war, 10,000 Orcs are marching toward his refuge, and he is only informed of this by Aragorn, who just happens to see the army on his way to the fortress. Meanwhile, Faramir has the greatest scouts in Middle-earth. They not only watch the borders of Gondor, they also check out what's happening in Rohan, hundreds of leagues away!

The Men are commanded to "fire" their arrows. However, this doesn't make any sense for a pre-firearm culture. Aragorn correctly says, "Release arrows."

Gimli must have bought "Hooked on Elvish." In the extended edition of the first film he asks Haldir to stop speaking Elvish because he can't understand it. In this film, he has no problem with "*pendraith*," the Elvish word for ladders.

In the theatrical cut, as Faramir and his captives approach Osgiliath, Minas Tirith cannot be seen. It should be in front of the mountains. (In test screenings, people confused Minas Tirith with Helm's Deep, so Minas Tirith was intentionally left out. It is present in the extended edition.)

Arwen was filmed arriving and fighting at Helm's Deep, but when the writers decided she shouldn't be there after all, her footage was edited out . . . mostly. She appears to the right of Éomer for half a moment in an establishing shot before the film cuts to a close-up of Éomer hacking away at Orcs.

In the book *The Two Towers*, Pippin talks about being captured by the Orcs. "Only nine days ago," he says. "It seems a year since we were caught." Unfortunately this line did not make it into the film, where it would have been amusing considering the release dates of the theatrical cuts.

The End of Other Things

A Nazgûl arrives at Osgiliath, but fails to capture Frodo or the Ring. Faramir, realizing the importance of Frodo's quest, lets the hobbit go. Frodo, Sam, and Gollum continue on to Mordor.

A stream in Ithilien searches for the Anduin River. (Dino Olivieri)

What the Big Folk Were Saying

"He has to be talking about that Elf witch from the first movie!"
— A man upon hearing Gollum say, "She might help"

What the Wizards Know

McKellen needed no persuading to let a stunt rider take his place on Shadowfax. His friend Roy Kinnear, a character actor, died after falling from a horse while filming *The Return of the Musketeers* (1989).

While filming the last scene with Frodo, Sam, and Gollum, members of the filming crew were required to wear hard hats due to the danger of falling pinecones. Astin, who had already been hit in the head by an Elven loom, obviously could not wear one, much to his dismay.

Gino Acevedo did seven years of makeup for The Lord of the Rings. *He appears as a Dwarf lord in the prologue of* The Fellowship of the Ring *and as a corsair pirate in* The Return of the King. (Ian Smith)

Makeup artist Gino Acevedo had to hide behind Rhys-Davies and keep hold of a string attached to the forehead makeup piece to hold it in place for the scene in the extended edition where Gimli and Legolas argue about who won the Orc slaying contest.

When Jackson and Walsh began to write the screenplays for these films, they were overwhelmed by the complexity of *The Lord of the Rings.* They asked Walsh's ex-boyfriend, Stephen Sinclair, for help, and he joined the writing team. Sinclair was not a big fan of the books and brought a bold new approach to the process, making big changes to Tolkien's story to make it more cinematic. Although Sinclair left the project before New Line Cinema acquired it (and *The Two Towers* became a standalone film), he does get a writing credit at the end as a thank you for his work, which showed Jackson and Walsh that deviations could greatly aid the films.

While working with Jackson and Walsh, Sinclair asked his girlfriend, Philippa Boyens, who knew the books better than he, for help. She became such an asset, she was asked to join the project as a script editor. As Sinclair became disinterested with the project (eventually leaving), Boyens filled the void, joining the writing team and helping Jackson and Walsh the rest of the way.

Jackson said *The Two Towers* was the most difficult of *The Lord of the Rings* films to write.

The filmmakers wanted "Gollum's Song" to be sung by Björk. When she turned it down because she was pregnant, Emilíana Torrini was brought in to perform the song in Björk's style.

What the Elvish Eyes and Ears Have Noticed
Unlike in the book, Frodo and the Ring are discovered by a Nazgûl at Osgiliath. This becomes very important in the third film.

Emilíana Torrini sings "Gollum's Song." (Minh Le)

Sam must have read *The Lord of the Rings*, because he says, "It's all wrong. By rights, we shouldn't even be here." In the books, Frodo and Sam never visit Osgiliath.

Sam's touching speech about the tales that really matter gives credit to the folk that go on when they have a chance to turn back. In *The Goonies* (1985), the protagonists, deep underground, are offered an opportunity to abandon their quest and safely make it back home. Mikey (Astin) gives a touching speech that convinces all to continue.

When Pippin discovers an apple at Isengard in the extended edition, he looks up, just like the first film. (He probably wants to make sure nobody is throwing anything at him.)

As the story is coming to a close, we get a short scene with our heroes on horseback, setting the stage for the battle of Middle-earth. There's the regal Aragorn, and to his left the Elvish Prince Legolas. Beside them, we have the wise Gandalf and lordly Théoden, with Gamling behind. And to their left we have the unforgettable . . . random guy who doesn't appear anywhere else in these films. (Guess who doesn't get a close-up.) If this were *Star Trek*, he'd be wearing a red shirt and meet some painful death in the opening of the next film.

Just like its prequel, this film sets up its sequel by telling us (through Gollum) exactly where Sam and Frodo will be going to next.

Jackson's *The Two Towers* is the only film adaptation of one of Tolkien's books where the Ring is never used.

The Foolishness of a Took

Curiously, while capturing Frodo and holding him against his will, Faramir never takes the hobbit's sword away.

When Éowyn hugs Aragorn, he's in his wet river clothes. That's because the shot was stolen from earlier in the film: from just after Aragorn arrives at Helm's Deep. The filmmakers must have decided to move the hug to later in the film.

In the extended edition, Gimli seems to have a bit too much of an understanding of the central nervous system for the time period he lives in.

In the extended edition credits, they misspell John Noble's name in the crawl. Imagine Boromir having to say, "My father is a Nogle man."

In 2002 the Academy gave *The Fellowship of the Ring* an Oscar for Best Original Score. In 2004 they gave the same honor to *The Return of the King*. Yet because of a confusing rule, the score for *The Two Towers* was not nominated, despite being declared eligible.

The Lord of the Rings Shooting Timeline

In late 1999 and throughout 2000, principal photography for *The Lord of the Rings* took place concurrently in New Zealand — as if the films were one large production. Whenever the actors were available in New Zealand in the years that followed, pickup shots were conducted.

This was a complex shoot. Dealing with scale issues, digital effects, and blue screen work meant that different parts of the same scene would sometimes be shot months apart or in different ways at different locations. Bad weather was also a factor and sometimes caused changes in the days' plans. However, the following is the basic schedule the shoot followed:

1999

September

(The Hobbit leads, along with Stuart Townsend and Orlando Bloom, arrived for training.)

October

(Filming began with Hobbit leads)

The Wooded Road/Encounter with Nazgûl

(Townsend departed)

Buckleberry Ferry

Bree Exterior

Amon Sûl (Weathertop)

(Viggo Mortensen arrived)

Isengard Deforestation

November

(Sean Bean arrived)

Anduin River/Argonath

Battle at Amon Hen (Breaking of the Fellowship)

December

Boromir's Death

Frodo's Escape from Boromir

Ford of Bruinen by Rivendell

Prancing Pony Interior

Exiting Moria

Approach to Lothlórien

2000

January

(Ian McKellen arrived)

Hobbiton

Grey Havens

Farmer Maggot's Field

Edoras

February

(Ian Holm and Christopher Lee arrived)

Bag End Interior

Orthanc Interior

Helm's Deep

March

Helm's Deep Continued

Gandalf at Orthanc

Rivendell Exterior

April

Helm's Deep Continued

Last Alliance (Prologue)

Aragorn and Gondor at the Black Gate

Caves of Orthanc

(*Andy Serkis arrived*)

Frodo and Sam in Mordor

May

Helm's Deep Concluded

Frodo and Sam in Mordor Concluded

Frodo, Sam, and Gollum at the Black Gate

Moria

Rivendell Interior

June

Paths of the Dead

(Cate Blanchett arrived)

Lothlórien

July

(Jackson's scheduled vacation that never happened)

Lothlórien concluded

Isengard

Cirith Ungol

August

Anduin River

Flooded Isengard

September

Caradhras

Voice of Saruman

Edoras

October

Edoras

Battle of the Pelennor Fields

November

Fangorn Forest

December

Fangorn Forest Concluded

Minas Tirith

2001

Pickup shots for *The Fellowship of the Ring*

2002

Pickup shots for *The Two Towers*

2003

Pickup shots for *The Return of the King*

2004

Pickup shots for *The Return of the King* extended edition

Q&A
with Zac the Orc

Zac was a mere Orc in *The Lord of the Rings*. Yet, to be only such is held worthy by us Ringers. His relationship with Jackson and Weta goes back to the days of *The Frighteners* (1996), and he's presently carving his own path in the industry as a scriptwriter and actor. On October 25, 2003, just after participating in the pick-up shots for the third film, he shared his thoughts with me.

Braun: How did you become involved with *The Lord of the Rings*?
Zac: I have an agent and was rung during the 2002 pickup shots. But as I had just started a new job, I turned it down. I had sworn off doing any further extra work after *The Frighteners*. This year I was again rung up (to be an Orc), so thought I might as well give it a go. I went in on my day off, loved it so much I resigned my work, and have been doing what I love ever since. At some point in one's life, one has to follow one's passion to happiness, success, and fulfillment, or languish in the Valley of Regret forevermore.

Braun: Had you read the books?
Zac: No, I only read *The Hobbit* as a kid, but deliberately stayed away from *The Lord of the Rings* when it was announced back in 1998. I wanted to see if I could follow the story without having any preconceptions or expectations. Mostly, seeing the films, it worked. But I didn't see the need for the octopus thing (the Watcher) at the time and still don't. What amazed me with *The Fellowship of the Ring* was the whole "wow" factor, as of course, it was all new to me. When the camera swoops down into the Orc caves, I wanted it to slow down, so I could take in all that was going on. The way to handle it was to see it a few more times. With *The Two Towers*, I loved how it leapt straight into the story and didn't let up. With *The Return of the King*, you will see a battle that will make Helm's Deep look like a child's tantrum in comparison. But you will also be very moved by the emotional content, as Jackson really piles on the tension/danger, etc. And the Mount Doom sequence . . . well, best bring a box of tissues with you.

Braun: What parts of *The Lord of the Rings* were you involved with?

Zac: The Battle of the Pelennor Fields, Minas Tirith, and the Gates of Mordor. Mostly either marching toward Minas Tirith, fleeing from the Spectrals, or a bit of fighting on the fields.

Braun: How did you prepare for shooting?

Zac: The general Orc costume consisted of a Lycra body suit, thermal wear if you wanted them, then trousers, two tops (one short– and one long–sleeved), and boots. After wardrobe, you walked over to Weta and were assigned your mask, a helmet, and pair of gloves. Then back to makeup to have the prosthetic (glue) makeup applied. This was "raccoon" rings around the eyes, mouth, and sometimes across the bridge of the nose, to hide the pink flesh from showing through the mask. Then over to catering for breakfast, and chill out until you were called to set. The actors who were close-up Orcs had their makeup applied in the makeup bus, as they had prosthetic attachments to wear and contact lenses. Then as you went on set, you were given a weapon to wield and sometimes a shield to carry. Then you had to *run* for it!

Often there was an indoor unit shooting as well as the outdoor one (Pelennor Fields for most of the time I was involved). The call time varied from 5 a.m. to 7 a.m. Occasionally later. Here, it is twelve hours work before overtime applies.

Braun: What was it like on set?

Zac: The first thing that struck me was how incredibly well organized it was. After four years, one would certainly know what worked and what didn't.

The Helm's Deep battle was hell, and I am so glad I wasn't there. It was filmed out at Hayward's Quarry (which, incidentally, is not too far from where I live) and the call time was 5:15 p.m. till around 7 a.m. or 8 a.m. the next morning. Most people live in town so had to leave earlier to beat the rush-hour traffic, then it was the reverse coming home. So it made for long days. It was originally meant to film for three weeks; it ended up being sixteen!

One night, when it was very chilly and a southerly wind was blowing (which comes up from Antarctica), they had done several takes with the rain tower, and a freak gust of wind came up and blew one of the towers over. A great Rohan cheer went up. But even the Uruk-hai didn't have it easy, as they wore prosthetic arms and legs, made from a sponge foam latex that soaked up water like a sponge.

Braun: What was it like when you were participating?

Zac: Sometimes it was hard work — marching over and over, or fleeing the CG elements that are added later. An enormous amount of footage was shot using variations to give Pete a wider choice in the editing suite. This is something I have noticed since being on *The Frighteners*. Not only was a take done however many times it was required, but they sectioned us off into small areas and filmed again and again using the MoCon camera (Motion Control) to do repeated passes, thus building up the numbers of Orcs. Usually there were about seventy to eighty of us; in the film up to 200,000. Magic, huh?

Jackson directed some of our scenes, but when he was in England editing the final cut, staff from Weta Digital did the directing, explaining to us each time what was occurring in the on-screen action. Frequently, this meant a foreground scene that had been shot months earlier. For example, Legolas hanging onto the leg of the Mûmak (that scene from the trailer), well, we did the background part of it a few weeks ago. Kinda weird, but a fascinating process.

Braun: You know it's a big movie project when all this is happening for pickup shots.
Zac: Gimli's stunt double is an acquaintance of mine. He said he was flown all over the country to work, and had three months of reshoots this year alone. Several times this was as a stunt co-coordinator, which meant he could stay in civvies instead of being made up and put in costume.

Braun: How did the film crew treat you?
Zac: Consideration was always given to our well-being; not only did the assistant directors carry the cups of water to keep us cool between the shots, but at times, anyone onhand would help out, take "heads off" (the foam latex masks we wore), or put them on, including the producer Barrie Osbourne! This, I believe, stems from the close-knit nature of Kiwi filmmakers and the can-do attitude we have. As far as the catering, the food was wonderful. Breakfast and lunch were provided, and all you needed to eat later that night at home was maybe a cookie for supper, and that was it.

Braun: I've been told this project was like Bilbo's birthday celebration: the scope of Bilbo's party is large, and requires so many supplies, all of Hobbiton is involved with it. *The Lord of the Rings* project must have affected New Zealand in a similar way.
Zac: Very much so. We are a small nation of only four million people, with a pioneering attitude that is a descendent from our ancestors' days of arrival to New Zealand. The do-it-yourself (DIY) attitude is a real Kiwi institution, if not mythical one. Almost everyone is a handyman, except me! But yes, apart from the now near-legendary making of the chain mail plastic rings by hand by an elderly couple

(a few million of them), much if not all of *The Lord of the Rings* was built from scratch. Even the locations were an open call for people to send in photos of places New Zealand–wide that they thought would be of use in the films. And there were those who sent or wanted to loan various bric-a-brac like candelabra for the films. At one point, it seemed as though everyone knew someone who was either involved directly (crew, actors, or extras) or making something for the films. You know about the so-called six degrees of separation? Well, here it is referred to as one degree!

The Return of the King

(2003)

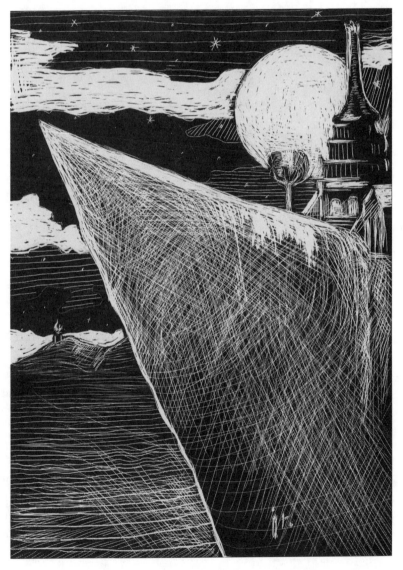

(Jacquie Roland)

Directed by: Peter Jackson

Starring:

Viggo Mortensen as Aragorn

Elijah Wood as Frodo

Sean Astin as Sam

Theatrical Cut: 3 hours 20 minutes

Ian McKellen as Gandalf

Rated PG-13

Miranda Otto as Éowyn

Released December 17, 2003

Bernard Hill as Théoden

Orlando Bloom as Legolas

Extended Cut: 4 hours 12 minutes

Andy Serkis as Gollum

Rated PG -13

John Rhys-Davies as Gimli

Released December 14, 2004

David Wenham as Faramir

John Noble as Denethor

Domestic Gross: $377,027,325

Billy Boyd as Pippin

Worldwide Gross: $1,119,263,306

Dominic Monaghan as Merry

The Return of the King is about the rebirth of hope and the return of majesty. It follows the story of the Ring from its reemergence from the Anduin River to its fate at Mount Doom while simultaneously following the threads of the Fellowship to their conclusion as well.

Everything about this film — the scope, the stakes, the finality, the running time — is bigger than *The Fellowship of the Ring* and *The Two Towers*. After starting the journey in the first film with just Frodo and Sam, by the third film we're following the fates of kings, armies, and kingdoms — like we've finally pulled back to see the entire sweeping vista of Middle-earth before us. And yet the emotional core of the story is not overwhelmed. Like Tolkien before him, who seemed to improve with every book he wrote, Jackson learned from *The Fellowship of the Ring* and *The Two Towers*, and applied the lessons when putting together this magical marathon.

Weaknesses? The film has few. Perhaps the last half is so exciting and emotionally draining that it is difficult for the viewer to have anything left when the fate of the Ring is revealed. However, in a world where we are charged more and more money for less and less entertainment, it's a small price to pay.

The truth is *The Return of the King* is so amazing it can't even be described, only experienced. Grab a comfortable chair. Take the phone off the hook. Find a hanky. *The Return of the King* makes *The Lord of the Rings* the one trilogy to rule them all.

The cast of The Lord of the Rings *celebrates the final film.* (Ian Smith)

Gollum's Story

Sméagol murders his best friend for the One Ring, which gradually transforms him into Gollum. Centuries later, he tells Frodo and Sam they are very close to Mordor, and beckons them to keep moving.

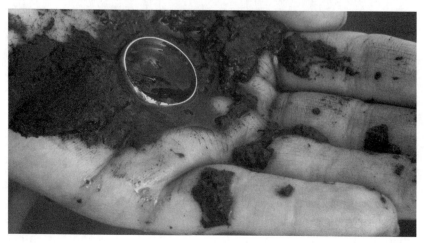

The Ring discovers the race of Hobbits. (J.W. Braun)

What the Big Folk Were Saying

"That's what I'm *Tolkien* about! Ha ha ha."

    — A teenage boy who thought he was so funny he had to repeat it throughout the film — and laugh at his own joke every time

"Is he turning into the Grinch?"

    — Woman as Sméagol transforms into Gollum

What the Wizards Know

Ever since Bob Shaye, head of New Line Cinema, made the decision to expand *The Lord of the Rings* from two to three films, many have assumed the decision was based on the fact that there are three books, even quoting Shaye as saying as much. However, according to Shaye himself, he never said — or cared about — anything of the sort. He turned two into three because of New Line Cinema's need for more sequels, and the idea that three years of business were better than two.

After living in Gollum's shadow, Serkis (right) finally gets some screen time at the beginning of The Return of the King. (Ian Smith)

The opening "*Lord of the Rings*" title shot was, again, simply borrowed from the first film.

Back when Arwen was to be at the battle of Helm's Deep, the script had this film open with a romantic moment between Aragorn and Arwen in the Glittering Caves the morning after the battle.

Serkis was initially cast as just the voice of Gollum. It was not until later that he was chosen to play the untransformed Sméagol.

Serkis directed much of the opening scene of *The Return of the King* himself when a director wasn't available.

With each successive film, the gap in time between principal photography and the pickup shoots increased. Early in this film, shots of Wood and Astin from 1999 are mixed with shots of the two from 2003.

What the Elvish Eyes and Ears Have Noticed

Déagol calls his friend, "Sméag." This isn't described in the book, yet it's perfectly plausible and especially jarring. To think of Sméagol as a fishing buddy you can call "Sméag" truly drives home how much he has changed by the time he meets Bilbo, Frodo, and Sam.

As Déagol looks at the ring, we can hear the sound of the woodland creatures fleeing — the same sound effect as in *The Fellowship of the Ring* when the Nazgûl approaches the Hobbits on the Wooded Road.

For the third film, Gollum's look was upgraded once again: His facial muscles, in particular, are more realistic than in the previous films.

The Foolishness of a Took

As Sméagol turns into Gollum, he loses most of his teeth. Yet, the Gollum we know and love has quite a few teeth. Perhaps Gollum loses his "good" teeth to make room for the Ring's preference of Evil teeth, like losing baby teeth to make room for adult molars.

Isengard and Edoras

Gandalf and company reunite with Merry and Pippin at Isengard before returning to Edoras to celebrate the victory over Saruman.

Edoras was filmed at New Zealand's Mount Sunday. (Ian Smith)

What the Big Folk Were Saying

"Hello? No, I can't talk now, I'm watching a movie. Call me back in a couple of hours."

— A man, apparently unaware of film's running time, or not caring about disturbing the theater later on

What the Wizards Know

The watery scene at the base of Orthanc was shot at the same location used for the Doors of Moria and the Dead Marshes.

The horses had to be filmed at the location over the course of three days. By the last day, the horses had had enough of standing in water and were quite ornery.

Jackson said that in retrospect, he should have put "The Voice of Saruman," a scene that appears at the beginning of *The Return of the King* extended edition and finishes Saruman's part in the tale, at the end of *The Two Towers* extended edition. He did not feel it was important enough to be in a theatrical cut.

What the Elvish Eyes and Ears Have Noticed

When Gandalf arrives at Isengard, the ancient Treebeard greets him as "Young Master Gandalf." I realize Treebeard has been around for a while, but Gandalf is what, three million years old?

Just afterward, Théoden's horse fertilizes Isengard. After what Rohan has been through you can't blame him. (Actually, due to the water, the cast and crew had a hard time keeping most of the horses from doing their business.)

Composer Shore makes a cameo appearance in the extended edition as a happy man of Rohan while Gimli and Legolas discuss their drinking game. (He's the guy on the left who gets a big laugh out of "no regurgitation.")

When Éowyn offers Aragorn a drink from the goblet, the image is a duplication of a painting by Alan Lee, with Otto's hair styled to match. *Lady Éowyn and Aragorn Take Leave* was painted to depict the parting of the two characters before Aragorn takes the Paths of the Dead, but Jackson shifted the image to earlier in the story.

The Foolishness of a Took

We saw how Gandalf reached the top of Orthanc in the first film. Saruman's a wizard, so I can understand how he can get to a place with no stairs or ladders. But how did Wormtongue get up there in the extended edition of this film?

Treebeard moves quickly. He begins and ends the Saruman scene in the extended edition in front of Orthanc's door. Yet throughout the scene, he's gone. (If Saruman is going to hurl flames at his guests, I don't blame him.)

The houses of Edoras have interesting chimneys. When we see them for the first time in this film, smoke pours into them rather than out. It's almost like a pull-out shot meant for *The Two Towers* has been reversed and used as a pull-in shot here.

The closed captioning says Éowyn is speaking in Elvish when she says, "*Westu Aragorn hál.*" However, she's speaking Rohirric. (I can just imagine the closed captioning people reading this book and saying, "Look, we did our best.")

The Animated Trilogy

You kids and your fancy newfangled *Lord of the Rings* films with their continuity and special effects . . . you don't know how good you have it! Back when I was a youngster, when we wanted to watch Tolkien movies, we had to watch the "animated trilogy": a collection of movies made by different companies, meaning that with each installment the characters, tone, and even the styles would change. One minute we'd be watching a four-foot girly Frodo, and the next thing you know, he's a two-foot-tall Orson Bean. Continuity? They couldn't even match up the ending of one film with the beginning of the next! And if someone said, "Hey, let's get Casey Kasem to do the voice of Merry!" did we have Peter Jackson to look out for us and say, "No, he'll sound too much like Shaggy from Scooby Doo"? No siree, Bob (or Nob). If the filmmakers wanted to have a junior high boys choir to sing at Lothlórien or have a warbling Minstrel of Gondor sing a ballad about the importance of rest while showing us images of happy, smiling Orcs waving hello to Hobbits, we just had to live with it, damn it. And did we complain? Well, yes. But truth be told, while the animated films might have some flaws, they're also a lot of fun too.

The Hobbit (1977), **76 minutes:** Rankin/Bass Productions (of *Rudolph the Red-Nosed Reindeer* fame) worked for five years and spent three million dollars on this animated adaptation for television. The studio had perfected a system for producing specials by this time: the hero is quickly introduced, sent on a quest, and must work his way through a series of musical numbers before finally achieving his goal. Because Tolkien's first book fits into this formula rather well, the movie isn't bad. The

Bilbo prepares for his "greatest adventure" in the animated adaptation of The Hobbit.
(The Rick Goldschmidt Archives)

animation, however, is dated, and the Rankin/Bass style isn't everyone's cup of tea. A funny note: this *Hobbit* was nominated for the 1978 Hugo Award for Best Dramatic Presentation but lost to *Star Wars* (1977). Tolkien would get his revenge, however. Peter Jackson's trilogy swept the award for three years while the *Star Wars* prequels were shut out.

The Lord of the Rings (1978), 133 minutes: While Rankin/Bass was preparing *The Hobbit*, Ralph Bakshi was creating a much deeper, darker, and more serious animated film based on *The Lord of the Rings* while suffering through a studio shakeup, budget problems, and a midstream change in producers and writers. Bakshi combined the technique of rotoscoping, where live actors were filmed in black and white and then drawn over by animators, with watercolor-like matte paintings to bring Middle-earth to life in a unique way. As mentioned elsewhere in this book, the wheels fall off the wagon when this film gets to

Saul Zaentz and Ralph Bakshi present a poster to the Swedish. (Victoria Bakshi Yudis)

The Two Towers, and the story ends rather abruptly with no resolution. Yet there's a lot of good stuff before then. There are moments where Bakshi proves *The Lord of the Rings* story can entertain on the big screen, mixed, of course, with the other moments that prove the '70s were not the time for a definitive adaptation of *The Lord of the Rings* to be made.

The Return of the King (1980), 98 minutes: Even before NBC aired the Rankin/Bass version of *The Hobbit* (and over a year before Bakshi's film was released), Arthur Rankin Jr. and Jules Bass began work on an adaptation of the last volume of *The Lord of the Rings* as a direct sequel to their prior romp in Middle-earth. This made-for-television movie focuses almost exclusively on Tolkien's three chapters about Frodo and Sam in Mordor. (Indeed, Aragorn doesn't have any lines until after Frodo has put the Ring on at Mount Doom.) There is also a musical number every few minutes. Because *The Fellowship of the Ring* and *The Two Towers* were skipped over, the result is a story that often provides short summarizations of hundreds of pages of exposition before launching you right into the payoff. There are some scenes that work well, giving us another hint that this Tolkien guy wrote some stuff that really does work cinematically, however it's also apparent that Rankin/Bass bit off too much to chew here.

The Villain, the Fool, and the Daughter

Gollum holds another debate with himself, but Sam discovers his evil intentions. Pippin steals the *palantír* and learns of Sauron's intentions. Arwen has a vision of her son and returns to Rivendell, where she confronts Elrond.

Andúril, the sword of the King, is forged from the shards of Narsil.

(J.W. Braun)

What the Big Folk Were Saying

"I thought he was about to make a call from his cell phone."
— Someone when Aragorn walks out of Meduseld to fill his pipe

What the Wizards Know

The Gollum/Sméagol debate by the pool was written and filmed before the Gollum/Sméagol debate that appears in *The Two Towers.*

The scene with Aragorn and Legolas looking out at the stars was a pickup shot, but Mortensen and Bloom were not filmed at the same time. Bloom was shot first and had departed New Zealand by the time Mortensen arrived to film his half of the scene. (Ironically, in an interview with Bloom at the films' official website, a still of this scene was used next to a question about what it was like to spend so much time with Viggo Mortensen!)

The scriptwriters knew Frodo would be the lead Hobbit in these films. They knew Sam would be his heavyset companion. They also had a handle on Pippin, knowing he's the character that's always getting into trouble. What the writers didn't know was what to do with Merry. They thought perhaps he could be the one to get Pippin into trouble before getting him out of it, which is hinted at in the extended edition of *The Return of the King*. But really, it was Monaghan who ended up defining the character.

In principal photography, Monaghan was shot saying, "We shall see the Shire again," as Merry and Pippin are about to separate. The line even appears in the film's trailer. The separation was reshot in 2003 with new dialogue when the writers decided Merry and Pippin should have more insecurity at this point and part on a sadder note.

Frodo, Sam, and Gollum's last scene in *The Two Towers* and Arwen's first scene in this film were shot in the same forest. (It has since been cut down — no doubt by Orcs.)

The sequence with Arwen departing, having a vision, and returning to Rivendell was intended to be in *The Two Towers*, and Tyler recorded "Arwen's Song" to serve as its score. But the filmmakers decided it would be better to end that film without showing the audience that Arwen is coming back, and shifted the sequence into *The Return of the King*. Furthermore, they thought it was awkward to hear Arwen singing over the top of her own scene. They had Shore compose another song: "Twilight and Shadow," which was sung by Renée Fleming.

Aragorn and Arwen's son, Eldarion, was played by Sadwyn Brophy. Sadwyn is the son of Orc, Nazgûl, and Rider of Rohan Jed Brophy.

After watching the first film, some fans became infatuated with an unnamed Elf at the Council of Elrond played by Bret McKenzie. As he can be seen just after Frodo agrees to take the Ring to Mount Doom, the fans gave him the name Figwit: "Frodo is great . . . Who is that?!" After becoming aware of the attention the extra was given, Jackson decided to use Figwit for a pickup scene shot in 2002. The Elf asks Arwen not to delay in *The Return of the King*. There have since been two Topps Trading Cards bearing his fan-derived name and an hour-long documentary about the phenomenon. McKenzie is now better known to mainstream audiences as one half of the New Zealand comedy duo, Flight of the Conchords. The novelty act, which includes Jemaine Clement, has a self-titled series on HBO, and in the show's first season, they paid homage to Bret's Elf past with the hilarious song, "Frodo, Don't Wear the Ring."

What the Elvish Eyes and Ears Have Noticed

When Pippin stares into the *palantír*, Sauron says, "I see you," just as he says to Frodo in the first film. This must be his catchphrase.

Gandalf, in surprise, exclaims, "Pippin!" when he discovers the Hobbit has looked into the *palantír*. While he sometimes uses a Hobbit's nickname when talking to someone else ("Sam has hardly left your side"), this is the only time in the trilogy he uses a Hobbit's nickname when directly addressing the Hobbit in question.

While Gandalf talks to Théoden in Meduseld about Pippin, someone walks a dog through the background in the first shot. This isn't odd . . . until the same person and dog walk by again a few moments later. They must be doing laps.

In the books, Aragorn uses the *palantír* to reveal himself to Sauron just after Gandalf takes Pippin away, and Sauron, not wanting to see the King of Gondor reclaim his throne, responds by attacking Minas Tirith. This film, however, doesn't contain this plot point, shifting Aragorn's use of the *palantír* to later in the story. So why does Sauron attack Minas Tirith, a move that catches Gandalf by surprise? We need only look at the end of the *The Two Towers* when Frodo is discovered at Osgiliath, with his Gondor friends, by the Nazgûl. Sauron believes Gondor has the Ring, and he's trying to reclaim it!

Miranda Otto (Éowyn) is welcome to take down a Nazgûl for me anytime. (Robert Millard/ Zuma Press/ Keystone Press)

Ever wonder what Elrond does at Rivendell when he's not manipulating his daughter or entertaining Hobbits and Dwarves? We find out in this film when Arwen surprises him with her return. He fills out paperwork! No doubt his average day is spent paying bills, working out schedules, balancing the books, that sort of thing.

When Arwen retrieves Narsil in the Grand Chamber of Rivendell, she walks past a mural of Ost-in-Edhil. After seeing this city's ruins in the first film, we now see what it looked like in its full glory.

The Foolishness of a Took

In the extended edition, Éowyn finds the most uncomfortable couch in Meduseld to sleep on after the victory celebration. Isn't her own bed somewhere nearby? After all, this is where she lives! Perhaps she gave up her room for a guest, but I doubt that Théoden would really want his mega-hot, young, single niece to sleep in a public place with lots of drunken men around.

When Merry asks Gandalf to help Pippin during the *palantír* incident, Gandalf's pitcher is present in one shot and gone the next. (I suppose this is an easy trick for a wizard to pull off.)

Gandalf, referring to Sauron, says, "His defeat at Helm's Deep showed our enemy one thing." The wizard then goes on to list three or four things. And isn't it a stretch to say *Sauron* was defeated at Helm's Deep?

Oddly, Gandalf tells Aragorn to follow the river and look to the Black Ships, and Aragorn simply ignores him.

When Arwen is reading her book, there is a picture on the right-hand page. When she drops the book it has been replaced by words.

Gondor Calls, Rohan Answers

Gandalf takes Pippin to Minas Tirith. Gollum leads Frodo and Sam to a way into Mordor near Minas Morgul, from which Sauron sends an army to attack Osgiliath. The Beacons of Gondor are lit to summon aid, and Théoden vows that Rohan will answer. Sauron's army drives Faramir back to Minas Tirith.

Mount Mindolluin, the easternmost of the White Mountains and protector of Minas Tirith. (Diane Rooney)

What the Big Folk Were Saying

"Who is Gondor, again?"
  — A confused girl

"Is that a helicopter landing pad?"
  — A woman when the courtyard of Minas Tirith is shown

Cell phone going off
  — Just as Aragorn says, "Gondor calls for aid"

What the Wizards Know

The Minas Tirith set was the largest set ever built in the southern hemisphere. It was built at the same quarry as Helm's Deep.

Of the miniatures used, Minas Tirith was the largest. The model measured over six meters in diameter and included over a thousand buildings.

The model makers decided not to make the outer wall of Minas Tirith appear to be made of a hard, black stone as described in the book because it would have complicated melding the miniature into its surroundings.

Sean Connery was sent scripts and was asked if he was interested in the part of Gandalf. He declined because he said he didn't understand the story. (Can you imagine him in the role? "Keep it shecret, keep it shafe.")

Rhys-Davies auditioned for the part of Denethor. (Just think, Rhys-Davies and Bloom nearly ended up as father and son. Instead, they play best friends.)

The late Sir Edmund Hillary, a fan of *The Lord of the Rings* who conquered Mount Everest just before the books were published, visited with the cast while the scene of Sam and Frodo at the Crossroads was being filmed. (The Crossroads scene appears only in the extended edition.) Hillary also toured Weta Workshop.

In the original shoot, the Lord of the Nazgûl's helmet resembled Sauron's helmet (seen in the prologue of the first film). This similarity created confusion in test screenings, with it appearing in the third film that Sauron was leading his Orcs into battle against Gondor. The helmet was redesigned in 2003, and all the Chief Nazgûl's appearances were reshot.

The Minas Morgul set caught fire one night and was partially damaged.

The Art Department conceived that Minas Morgul would have a rookery for the Fell Beasts. However, like the stables of Helm's Deep, the rookery wasn't built and the audience is left to imagine it. (There's another one for you fan artists out there.)

Royd Tolkien, the great grandson of J.R.R. Tolkien, asked if he could have a quick look at the project. To his surprise, Jackson offered him a part in the films. You can see him handing out spears to the men at Osgiliath. Christopher Lee, experienced at meeting Tolkiens, took Royd out to dinner.

The scene with the Orcs crossing the Anduin required a set with water. So, as you might have guessed, it was filmed at the same location as a flooded Orthanc. And the Dead Marshes. And the Doors of Moria.

Two beacons were constructed. One was a set, and another was actually built at the top of a mountain, complete with a hut for the guards.

Kiran Shah, Wood's scale double for Frodo, had much more experience than the other scale doubles, having been an actor and a stuntman in blockbuster films such as *Superman* (1978), *The Dark Crystal*

Kiran Shah has been in eight or nine of my ten favorite films.
(Courtesy Kiran Shah)

(1982), *The Return of the Jedi* (1983), *Indiana Jones and the Temple of Doom* (1984), *Aliens* (1986), and *Titanic* (1997). Because of this, Shah played all four lead Hobbits as well as Bilbo at one time or another. He also served as a mentor to the other scale doubles, and came in handy when a tricky stunt was needed.

Gothmog sticking his spear into Madril and declaring it the time of the Orc was a pickup shot in 2003, and the last time actors were filmed for this project.

What the Elvish Eyes and Ears Have Noticed
The Rammas Echor, a great and ancient wall that is supposed to surround the Pelennor Fields, is absent in this adaptation.

When Pippin first meets Denethor, you can see the Rod of the Stewards to Denethor's right. It has been set aside, symbolic of Denethor setting aside his duties in the wake of Boromir's death. This heirloom is not to be confused with Rod Stewart, symbolic of the music industry selling out in the wake of slumping sales.

Jackson has a cameo as the bosun of the corsair ship, seen giving orders as Gandalf says, "All will answer Mordor's call."

Minas Morgul, once Minas Ithil, is architecturally similar to Minas Tirith, formerly its sister city.

The guardian statues of Minas Morgul should look familiar to fans of the first film. They're Balrogs!

Aragorn's hair makes a cameo appearance at Osgiliath. Royd Tolkien was given Mortensen's wig to wear.

The writers did a good job of connecting the separate storylines. Frodo and Sam, indeed, are just a few leagues from Gandalf and Pippin as they approach Minus Morgul (a fact that's difficult to realize when reading the books because of their structure), and so it makes sense that all four would see the same green signal. And

John truly is a Noble man, but I might have cast Denethor differently. (Ian Smith)

by connecting Minas Tirith to Rohan via the beacons, Gandalf and Pippin have their storyline interwoven with Aragorn and Merry. All this leads to a more cohesive story.

John Noble is fine as Denethor, but I can't help but wonder if somebody like Patrick Stewart or David Warner would have brought more gravitas, more complexity, and more respect to the role.

Gothmog, the Orc captain, looks like Sloth from *The Goonies* (1985). I half-expect to see Sean Astin come to his aid.

The famous film scream that has become an inside joke (see page 114) can be heard again just after Gandalf (with Pippin) rides out to rescue Faramir from the Nazgûl.

Pat Acton, a career and employment counselor, builds models out of matchsticks as a hobby. Acton, who doesn't know how to do things halfway (as a boy he built a tree-house that had painted siding, glass windows, and a heating stove) has used hundreds of thousands of matchsticks to build this model of Minas Tirith.

(Pat Acton)

The Foolishness of a Took

Oddly, Denethor's chamber is not topped by the White Tower as described in the book. In fact, the Tower has been moved off to the side, quite symbolic of the writers' decision to not use it in the story. The Sideshow Weta collectable model of Minas Tirith, included with *The Return of the King* Collector's Edition DVD set, has this tower leaning slightly to the left.

When the scene with Gandalf and Pippin in the guesthouse begins, Pippin is tucked in bed. In the next shot, Pippin is standing, and his Gondorian raiments and weapons are on the bed.

Gandalf reminds Pippin — and the audience — what happened at Weathertop (Amon Sûl). Unfortunately, unless someone has read

Ringers: Lord of the Fans

Ringers: Lord of the Fans is the best film you might not have heard about. In January 2002, Tolkien fans Cliff Broadway and Carlene Cordova met while standing in line to meet Ian McKellen at a book signing. The two began working together, interviewing the stars of *The Lord of the Rings* for the TheOneRing.net, an online community where fans can meet, chat, and get the latest news. As the two watched *The Lord of the Rings* films become a phenomenon, Broadway and Cordova began to think about incorporating their footage into a larger project. After assembling a team, they put together a stunning 97-minute documentary, narrated by Dominic Monaghan, about the history of Tolkien fandom and its impact on popular culture. The film was not released theatrically, but at the 2005 Slamdance film festival,

Ringers closes out its successful run at the Slamdance Film Festival.

(Carlene Cordova)

the book, he or she isn't going to recognize the name, because Weathertop is never mentioned in the first film.

As proven in the first film, a flame in the dark can be seen a long way away by unfriendly eyes. Why then in *Return of the King* do the Orcs carry torches when they cross the river? And why can't the Men see them?

When galloping off to battle the Nazgûl and rescue Faramir wouldn't it make more sense for Gandalf to leave Pippin behind? (In truth, when this scene was filmed, the script at that point had it as Gandalf and Pippin's arrival at Minas Tirith.)

fans made history by camping out overnight to buy tickets to see it; something that had never happened before in the festival's 11-year existence. Thankfully, you no longer need a sleeping bag. It is available at Netflix, or it can be purchased at www.ringerstore.com.

The Ringers *crew: from left to right, Nick Langley, Cliff Broadway, Angie Pop, Josh Mandel, John Welch.* (Carlene Cordova)

Faramir says goodbye to Frodo and Sam in the *The Two Towers*. In this film, Pippin asks how long it will take to get to Minas Tirith, and Gandalf says three days. Fair enough. But at Minas Tirith, I assume at least three days later, Faramir tells Gandalf he last saw Frodo and Sam less than two days ago. What? Either someone's math is off or the films' editors have been giving us these sequences out of order.

The Liar, the Madman, and the Dead

Denethor is upset with Faramir and sends him back to Osgiliath, even as the enemy plots to lay siege to Minas Tirith. Gollum drives a wedge between Sam and Frodo, prompting the hobbits to part. Aragorn, Legolas, and Gimli, following the advice of Elrond, take the Paths of the Dead. Meanwhile, Faramir is wounded and Minas Tirith is attacked.

The entrance to the Paths of the Dead was filmed at the Putangirua Pinnacles. (Tom Wuellette)

What the Big Folk Were Saying

"Hey, that's not supposed to happen."

— A man when Frodo tells Sam to go home

What the Wizards Know

In addition to playing Lurtz, Lawrence Makoare played both Gothmog and the Lord of the Nazgûl. Makoare enjoyed playing the Nazgûl the most, because the role didn't require any makeup or prosthetics. Weta Digital manipulated the image of the Nazgûl to make the character taller and thinner than Gothmog.

Craig Parker, who played Haldir, voiced a few characters in this film, including Gothmog and his evil lieutenant, the noseless Orc with a head on his helmet.

Monaghan, auditioning new members for Drive Shaft. (Ian Smith)

Serkis voiced the Lord of the Nazgûl.

The horses in Minas Tirith, like those at Helm's Deep, needed rubber horseshoes to avoid slipping.

The song Pippin sings for Denethor was composed by Boyd himself.

Monaghan never auditioned for the role of Merry. When the hundreds of people who did turned out to be unsatisfactory, Jackson and Walsh found Monaghan among the Frodo audition tapes they had filed away after Wood had gotten the part.

For the shot of the Evenstar pendant breaking on the floor, a new pendant was made that was five times the size of the original.

Remember the first shot of Gandalf — riding through a field in his cart on the way to Hobbiton? The same field reappears in this film as the thousands of Rohirrim depart for Gondor.

Sir James Galway, nicknamed "the Man with the Golden Flute" lent his talents to The Lord of the Rings. *His flute solo as Faramir departs Minas Tirith is one of the defining moments in the trilogy.*
(Simon Robertson)

Filming for the extended edition of *The Return of the King* concluded in 2004 — after the film had won its Oscar for Best Picture. The last piece of footage shot for the trilogy was at the Paths of the Dead: skulls roll at the feet of our heroes before the avalanche.

What the Elvish Eyes and Ears Have Noticed

As Frodo, Sam, and Gollum continue to struggle up the stairs (with Gollum eyeing up the Ring), the army continues to issue from Minas Morgul below them. As Martin Brody would say: Faramir, you're gonna need a bigger boat.

The children of Jackson and Walsh appear as "Cute Gondor Children" while Faramir and his men prepare to exit the Gates of Minas Tirith.

As Aragorn first looks toward the door under the mountain, the King of the Dead briefly appears.

It seems New Line Cinema didn't like the job the Elves did reforging the Sword of Kings. In the film, Andúril is a full two-handed sword. In the teaser poster, it has been digitally shortened.

In *The Return of the King* Elrond says in Elvish, "I give hope to Men," and Aragorn responds, "I keep none for myself." These two lines are the inscription on the grave of Aragorn's mother, seen in the extended edition of *The Fellowship of the Ring.*

When Brego flees from the door under the mountain, he takes Aragorn's scabbard with him, forcing Aragorn to carry his sword in his hand. In truth, this was to cover up the fact that the sword was too long for Mortensen to sheathe and unsheathe alone.

In the theatrical cuts the editing knife seems to have come down hardest on Lothlórien, Fangorn Forest, and the Paths of the Dead. This is because, by Jackson's own admission, these parts of the story would not have been included had he written an original screenplay. The extended editions include much more footage for each of these, greatly improving all three.

The Return of the King Easter Egg Alert

There is a hidden bonus feature included on the first disc of *The Return of the King* Platinum Series Special Extended Edition (the four disc set that comes in the blue box). It's a gag interview with Wood that is highly unsuitable for children. To access it, go to the "Select a Scene" menu and navigate to the final group of scenes. Then navigate down from Scene 36 to reveal a hidden Ring symbol and press "Enter."

In the book, the siege of Minas Tirith occurs mostly at night, like the battle at Helm's Deep. In the film, it's cloudy, but not always night. I like this change, because cinematically it breaks up the darkness, which would otherwise become monotonous.

The Troll drummers have rather good rhythm for an intellectually challenged species. Does Sauron allow them to participate in marching band classes, or are Trolls just naturally gifted?

The Foolishness of a Took

In the extended edition Denethor's stone chair wobbles when he falls backward onto it after yelling at Faramir.

Shelob and the Battle of the Pelennor Fields

Gollum leads Frodo into a trap; the hobbit is stung by a giant spider and captured by the enemy. The Siege of Minas Tirith continues, but Rohan and Aragorn arrive in succession to free the city, and Merry and Pippin reunite.

Sting and the Ring pass to a third hobbit. (J.W. Braun)

What the Big Folk Were Saying

"Oh, he is so dead! Dad, is he dead? Hey, he can't die."
— A boy when Frodo is stung by Shelob

"Bet she now wishes she'd stayed home like a woman should."
— Husband to his wife, when Éowyn, clearly frightened, prepares to battle (his wife gave him an icy glare in return)

Biggest laugh in the trilogy.
— When Gimli tells Legolas the Mûmak only counts as one

"Luke, tell your sister you were right about me."
— A man after Éowyn says she must save Théoden and Théoden replies she already did

What the Wizards Know

To make Shelob's cobwebs, two different polymers had to be heated to 220 degrees Celsius. At 228 degrees the mixture would burst into fire, as the crew found out firsthand.

The flaming "boulders" the Orcs hurl at Gondor were actually made of straw.

When Sam first approaches Shelob, Jackson's arm has a cameo: it is the director himself holding Sting in the shot just before Sam says, "Let him go, you filth."

The audition scene that netted Astin the part was of Sam talking to the unconscious Frodo after Shelob's attack.

During the shoot, a technician spotted what appeared to be David Wenham (Faramir), looking sickly, passed out on the floor. After trying to get Wenham something to drink, the technician was informed he was looking at a dummy made for the Faramir near-death experience, so Wenham wouldn't be needed for all the shots.

Of all the scenes in the trilogy, Rohan's arrival at Gondor required the most extras.

Bernard Hill is left-handed, and therefore Théoden is as well. However, the scene with Théoden rattling the spears of his men (which was Hill's idea) was blocked out in such a way that Hill had to hold his sword in his right hand.

The scene where Denethor pours oil on himself was Noble's last scene. It had to be, because the "oil" (which was actually a special compound made by the Art Department) wrecked the wig. (Thank goodness they didn't need a second take!)

Jackson's and Walsh's first treatment of *The Lord of the Rings*, written in 1997, describes Denethor's flaming demise precisely how it appears in the final film.

Billy Boyd's comic and dramatic timing are both so wonderful, he owns every scene he's in. (Ian Smith)

The corsair ships, including the one Aragorn, Legolas, and Gimli jump out of, were miniatures. In fact, the ships were all the same miniature, used over and over. The dock where the ships arrive was the last miniature built for the trilogy.

Legolas' big moment in this film, where he single-handedly takes down a Mûmak, was a pickup shot. His stunts in the prequels had been so well received, Jackson decided to add a grand finale.

Théoden's death was also a pickup shot. In fact, it was Hill's last shot, filmed after his farewell party.

Replaced by another piece of music, "Arwen's Song," recorded for Arwen's vision of her son, serves instead as the score for Éowyn's and Faramir's healing in the extended edition. It represents a sympathetic blessing from Arwen, who understands the difficulties of romance in the changing world.

The Lord of the Rings Film Trilogy
By the Numbers

100 locations were used

350 sets were created

18,000 costumes were created — not only were they all made from scratch, most of their fabrics were as well

114 speaking roles were cast

30 of those roles required training for fictional languages and dialects

430 people worked in the Art Department

20,602 background actors were used

48,000 props were used

250 real horses appear

21 unreal Mûmakil appear

8 Ent designs appear

9 hours and 17 minutes is the total running time of the theatrical cuts

Karl Urban (Éomer) insisted Éomer be present as his sister Éowyn is healed by Aragorn in the extended edition.

The dead Mûmak lying on the ground was the largest prop manufactured for these three films, and one of the largest props in film history. It was built in just twenty-one days.

The scene of Pippin finding Merry was switched from day to night many times during editing, before being cut from the theatrical edition . . . only to be reinstated as a day scene just before the film's premiere. In the extended edition it appears again, but as a night scene.

What the Elvish Eyes and Ears Have Noticed

I'm not sure what's more surprising — that Frodo tells Sam to go home, or that Sam turns around and begins to do so. It's not the

11 hours and 22 minutes is the total running time of the
    extended cuts
1600 to 2000 edits were necessary for each commentary track
    (included in the Platinum Series Special Extended Editions).
    Pellerin Multimedia had the cast and crew do multiple takes for
    each segment and used what they thought were best.
6 months is how long the commentaries took to complete.
$125 million was paid to Jackson for giving us *The Lord of
    the Rings*.

Visual Effects Shots
    560 appear in *The Fellowship of the Ring* theatrical cut
    620 appear in *The Fellowship of the Ring* extended cut
    720 appear in *The Two Towers* theatrical cut
    1000 appear in *The Two Towers* extended cut
    1450 appear in *The Return of the King* theatrical cut
    1800 appear in *The Return of the King* extended cut

breaking of the friendship that startles me, it's the destination. Is he really going to walk all the way back to Hobbiton? I hope he doesn't try to take the way he came, because the Mines of Moria aren't much use anymore.

Frodo loses the Phial of Galadriel when he slides down the hole Shelob can't fit through. He also loses his sword in a web.

Shelob's musical theme is, appropriately enough for an arachnid, an eight-note phrase.

The Lothlórien musical theme has an interesting journey in these films. In *The Fellowship of the Ring* it debuts with a somewhat frightening feel. In *The Two Towers* it sonically serves as a foreign friend at Helm's Deep. Here in *The Return of the King*, as Frodo turns to its light in his darkest hour, it has become a comforting companion.

Following the lead of the original books, the filmmakers separate the Hobbits into two groups, then split up both pairs so that each Hobbit is on his own, dealing with death and despair.

The dead Kings of Rath Dínen, the silent street, are positioned just like Aragorn was in Arwen's vision in *The Two Towers*.

Just like the description in the book, Grond has spells of ruin written on it in the Black Speech. Not described in the book, but fitting nonetheless, the Orcs have made many spelling mistakes.

The melody of "Into the West," the closing song, subtly plays as Gandalf describes the afterlife to Pippin.

Éowyn's slaying of the Lord of the Nazgûl is a very Hollywood moment. Rather than saying, "You look upon a woman," and warning him to depart, like the book, she waits until he's injured and says, "I am no man" in true "Hasta La Vista, Baby" style while preparing the death blow.

Before Legolas takes down the Mûmak, one of the Haradrim does a "Wilhelm" scream as he falls off.

The Foolishness of a Took
Éowyn isn't really experienced with this "incognito" business, is she? In the extended edition she takes off her helmet while on the way to Gondor.

After Sam stabs Shelob, he pulls his sword out. Then in the next shot . . . he pulls his sword out again!

According to the very miniature of Minas Tirith used in the films, Rath Dínen is located at the rear of the sixth level of the city. This means flaming Denethor has to run down the corridor leading back to the main levels, along the street to the tunnel leading to the Citadel, up the staircase, and (after turning 180 degrees) around the staircase and across the pier of rock to make his dive. He must be a very determined man.

When Éowyn is fighting the Lord of the Nazgûl, her helmet is strapped around her chin. However, the strap conveniently disappears when she dramatically pulls her helmet off.

The Land of Shadow and the Last Debate

Sam rescues Frodo from the Tower of Cirith Ungol. While Aragorn leads the Men of the West to the Black Gate to distract Sauron, Frodo and Sam journey to Mount Doom and destroy the Ring.

Mount Ruapehu was the perfect Mordor . . . usually. (Tom Wuellette)

What the Big Folk Were Saying

"Um . . . duh."

— A young girl when the group is discussing how to draw Sauron's Eye from Frodo, and Legolas says, "A diversion."

"Well, why not?"

— A pervy Hobbit-fancier when Sam says Frodo can't walk through Mordor in naught but his skin

What the Wizards Know

The part of the book where Sam has difficulty getting past the Two Watchers (which is in the Rankin/Bass adaptation) was shot but not used in Jackson's version, as it didn't advance the story.

Astin has cited the Tower of Cirith Ungol as his favorite set.

The last scene shot in principal photography was "The Last Debate," where Aragorn and company discuss creating a diversion to give Frodo a chance to destroy the Ring.

The Minas Tirith miniature had to be completely repainted to match the lighting of the live-action footage for when the Men of the West depart the city to challenge Mordor.

The filmmakers shot Faramir and Éowyn smooching and getting married, but left these parts out of the film, much to the dismay of Faramir/Éowyn shippers.

Mordor scenes were shot at Mount Ruapehu, an active volcano with a dry, rocky, desolate look. One morning, however, the crew found that Mordor had disappeared in the night. It had snowed, and Sauron's inhospitable domain looked more like a cheery winter wonderland. (I can't help but imagine the gleeful Orcs, celebrating after Sauron has declared a snow day, making snowmen and sledding down the slopes of Ephel Dúath. Wait, was that in the Rankin/Bass adaptation?)

The extras at the Black Gate, which was shot at a munitions training ground, were members of the New Zealand Army.

As Mortensen was filmed on his horse addressing the Men of the West, Weta workers hid behind the army, ducking down, so when the shot was finished they could help the extras with their armor.

Jackson has said that for him the defining moment in the trilogy is when Sam picks up Frodo and carries him up the volcano.

Tolkien considered having Pippin die at the Black Gate, but changed his mind.

Aragorn was filmed fighting Sauron in the final battle, but the writers had reservations about this, and Sauron was changed to a Troll.

Bloom's bow broke just as he was finishing Legolas' final shots for the final film.

The climactic struggle between Frodo and Gollum at the Crack of Doom was a 2003 pickup shot. In principal photography, the scene was shot with Frodo pushing Gollum off the ledge.

The Ring's destruction was the last approved visual effects shot for the theatrical cut, given the nod by Jackson days before the film premiered.

The lava bombs in the background after Mount Doom erupts were charcoal briquettes.

What the Elvish Eyes and Ears Have Noticed

You can see where Frodo was stung: just above his right breast. Had Shelob stung a bit lower, she would have hit Frodo's *mithril* shirt.

One of the Orcs could be a professional wrestler. He throws a WWE-style dropkick.

After being stuck in *The Two Towers* book for most of this film, Frodo and Sam finally enter *The Return of the King* when Sam storms the tower to rescue Frodo.

The film cuts from Pippin finding Merry to Sam rescuing Frodo. How's that for cool editing?

Sam stabs Gorbag, the Orc holding Frodo prisoner, and Sting stops glowing as Gorbag dies.

When Sam shows Frodo that he has taken the Ring for safekeeping, the score reverts to the same creepiness as when Sméagol and Déagol first discovered the Ring.

There's a great moment between the Hobbits as Sam gives the Ring back to Frodo. Sam, feeling the pull of the Ring, is reluctant to give it back. However, he tries to mask this temptation by making

Viggo Mortensen and Orlando Bloom create a diversion. (Robert Millard/ Zuma Press/ Keystone Press)

himself believe he simply doesn't want to burden Frodo with its weight. Frodo, going through "withdrawal," wants the Ring back like an addict wants a drug. However, he tries to mask this addiction by saying he's reclaiming the Ring so it won't destroy Sam.

Sam's about as bad at going incognito as Éowyn. Refusing to part with his cooking gear, he keeps it hitched to his belt while in Orc garb. How many Orcs walk around with frying pans? (Of course, this does give him the advantage of having extra weapons, considering he has used these pans to fight Orcs in the past.)

Quick, who becomes the Steward of Gondor after Denethor dies? Wrong! It's Gimli . . . or at least he's sitting in the Steward's chair during the "Last Debate" scene.

Gimli's line, "What are we waiting for?" reminds us of his introduction; he says this very line at the Council of Elrond as he attempts to destroy the Ring himself.

In the animated films of the '70s and '80s, Saruman has no palantír, but Denethor does. In Jackson's live-action films, the reverse is true.

In the theatrical cut of *The Return of the King*, there's a shot of a whipper ordering a marching army of Orcs to the Black Gate, which helps Frodo and Sam achieve their quest. This same shot is included in the extended edition, but in the latter cut, Frodo and Sam have been captured and are part of the army!

The Mouth of Sauron, seen in the extended edition, seems to me less like an Ambassador of Evil and more like a game show host.

When Sam picks up Frodo and ascends Mount Doom, Tolkien writes that Sam might have been given some gift of strength allowing him to take things to another level. I think the same gift was given to Howard Shore. At this point his score suddenly leaps from "fantastic" to "divine" as he carries the film to the closing credits and beyond.

We can see the metaphorical road Frodo is on, and where it goes, by looking back to earlier in the film when Gollum says, "We forgot the taste of bread, the sound of trees, the softness of the wind, we even forgot our own name."

The "Fellowship" musical theme, fragmented since the first film, suddenly returns to full glory as the remaining members of the company rush into battle "for Frodo."

Gandalf falls off a cliff in the first film, but he comes back. Aragorn falls off a cliff in the second film, then he comes back too. Gollum falls off a cliff in the third film, and surprise, guess who comes back? Did Wile E. Coyote write this script?

Frodo's look as he claims the Ring mirrors the shot of Isildur making the same choice in the first film.

When he regains the Ring, Gollum stands up straight for the first time.

When the Ring falls into the lava, its writing reappears. This is not described in the book, yet it's exactly what should happen as the Ring grows hot. The filmmakers deserve credit for realizing this.

The Ring does not give in to its destruction until Frodo chooses to be rescued, abandoning it.

The Foolishness of a Took
While fighting over Frodo's shirt, Shagrat tosses Gorbag against the wall, and Gorbag's wig comes off.

In the commentary track by the design team, John Howe says Tolkien never got around to explaining the agriculture of Mordor and how Sauron feeds his Orcs. I beg to differ. In the chapter "The Land of Shadow" in *The Return of the King,* Tolkien explains it in precise detail.

The End of All Things

Frodo and Sam prepare to die, but are saved by Gandalf. The remaining Fellowship members reunite and attend Aragorn's coronation before the Hobbits return to Hobbiton. A few years later, Frodo and the other Ring-bearers depart Middle-earth.

"How do you pick up the pieces of an old life?" (Tom Wuellette)

What the Big Folk Were Saying

"And it was all a dream! Ha ha ha!"

— A man when Frodo wakes up in Gondor

"I thought that would never end. Did it actually end? In fact, I think I'm still watching it."

— An older woman at the end

"Why didn't Frodo get to be king? That made me mad."

— A young girl to her friend

What the Wizards Know

The Return of the King was released December 17, 2003, exactly 100 years after the Wright Brothers made mankind's first powered flight. The date was also exactly three years after Wood, Monaghan, Boyd, Astin, McKellen, Mortensen, Bloom, and

Beattie got matching Fellowship tattoos. (Bean later got one too. Sean, not Orson.)

These films were nearly postponed by the return of a different king. As Miramax was negotiating with Zaentz to obtain the rights to go forward with *The Lord of the Rings*, Jackson was offered a chance to direct a remake of his favorite film, *King Kong* (1933) for Universal. But with *The Frighteners* (1996) performing poorly at the box office, and remakes of *Mighty Joe Young* (1998) and *Godzilla* (1998) going into production, Universal postponed plans for *King Kong*, leaving Jackson free to explore Middle-earth.

When *King Kong* was still a possibility in 1996, Miramax and Universal discussed working together by co-investing in *Kong*, then co-investing in *The Lord of the Rings*, and splitting the money the films made. Miramax, however, pointed out that *The Lord of the Rings* was (at that stage) two films, and asked for another Universal film to be part of the deal. Universal, in turn, placated Miramax by selling off a project that Universal thought was a money pit. The *Kong/Rings* partnership never materialized, but Miramax kept the rights to that other project, *Shakespeare in Love* (1998), which went on to win seven Academy Awards, including Best Picture.

When Aragorn's coronation was first filmed, the crown slipped right over Mortensen's brow, over his face, and fell down to his shoulders.

Aragorn sings the words Elendil spoke when his feet first touched the lands of Middle-earth. Aragorn's ancestor spoke of himself and his heirs remaining in Middle-earth for the rest of time. Mortensen thought Aragorn should sing this, as he does in the book, and he composed the tune himself.

Returning to Hobbiton was a happier experience for Frodo and Sam than for the actors. Wood couldn't control his pony and Astin was allergic to his.

McKellen's first day of shooting was Gandalf's arrival at Hobbiton. His second day of shooting was saying goodbye at the Grey Havens. As this point, he later admitted, he hardly knew Frodo from Merry.

The Grey Havens was reshot twice due to a wardrobe malfunction and focus problems.

Frodo was filmed looking sickly at the Grey Havens. Jackson later thought the hobbit should look healthier and had Frodo's look changed in postproduction.

Here's a little fun fact you can surprise your friends with: Frodo is played by a girl. No, not Frodo Baggins, but Frodo-lad, the baby Rosie holds. Sarah McLeod (Rosie) and Astin were filmed with their daughters for the closing scene.

After Galadriel was chosen as the narrator for the opening of *The Fellowship of the Ring*, the writers figured she would narrate the closing of the last film. Considering she also gives a monologue in the middle of *The Two Towers*, this would have been very symmetrical. The plan changed, however, when the editing of *The Return of the King* did not necessitate it. Still, Annie Lennox sounds like Galadriel, and the closing song can be considered Galadriel's closing thoughts.

Both Tolkien and the scriptwriters penned what happens to the other characters after the Frodo departs Middle-earth. However, each separately came to the conclusion to not use the material in their stories.

Before Annie Lennox recorded "Into the West," the closing song for this film, Shore asked her to record "Use Well the Days," a composition of his with lyrics adapted from Tolkien's books. While the latter song is not included in *The Lord of the Rings* films or soundtracks, Shore considered it an important part of his Middle-earth musical journey.

Peter Jackson knows how to close out a trilogy, and dominate the Oscars. (Ian Smith)

The portraits for the credits were McKellen's idea, reminiscent of old television shows that freeze-frame on characters smiling as their credit is given. Walsh, with the help of the Art Department, selected frames from the films representative of the way she wanted the characters to be remembered, and Alan Lee used them as the basis for pencil drawings. Other drawings from his sketchbook were then chosen to fill out the closing sequence.

You might wonder what Tolkien would have thought of these films. There were proposals for films during his lifetime, so we know some of his thoughts. He understood that a film adaptation required some changes to the story, though he wanted those changes to be well thought out and respect the original version. He wrote that the journey of the Ring-bearers should be the heart of the films. After the London premiere of *The Fellowship of the*

Ring, one of Tolkien's relatives approached Jackson and said her uncle would be very happy. It meant a lot to Jackson.

The Return of the King was the first fantasy film to win the Oscar for Best Picture.

What the Elvish Eyes and Ears Have Noticed

After seeing Sam completely devote himself to Mr. Frodo for most of the trilogy, it's "an eye-opener" to hear Sam speak of his own wishes and desires (such as Rosie Cotton) after the Ring is destroyed.

Because of Faramir, Gandalf knows Gollum has journeyed with Frodo and Sam. What he doesn't know is what has happened between these three at Mount Doom when it erupts. Therefore, Gandalf brings three eagles to rescue the survivors, thinking even of Gollum after all that has happened.

As the Eagles rescue Frodo and Sam, Elvish singing can be heard. The lyrics translate to: "In a dream I was lifted up from the darkness above rivers of fire. On wings soft as the wind. What's happened to the world? Is everything sad going to come untrue?"

The white light as Frodo awakens in Gondor mirrors his reunion with Gandalf at Rivendell.

After wearing increasingly dark colors throughout the trilogy, Arwen wears a green dress for her final scene, symbolizing the spring that has come to Middle-earth and to her life.

At Aragorn's coronation, the Hobbits are not wearing their original clothes, but special replicas made for the ceremony.

During the ceremony, you can see the mountains of Mordor behind the Hobbits as the people of Gondor bow before them. However, the mountains look quite different now with a blue sky overhead.

The map of Middle-earth in this film is nearly identical to the one seen at the beginning of the extended edition of *The Fellowship of the Ring*. Sharp-eyed fans, however, will note the two are not the same.

After traveling left to right on-screen on their way to Mordor, the Hobbits travel right to left on their way back to Hobbiton — and to the Grey Havens.

The children of Jackson and Walsh appear again as cute Hobbit children at Sam's wedding.

The shot of Frodo writing at Bag End mirrors the shot of Bilbo writing in the extended edition of the first film.

Bag End now has two swords and a crest hung up on the wall.

At the Grey Havens you can see Narya, one of the Three Rings for the Elven Kings, on Gandalf's hand.

The Grey Havens scene includes Círdan, last seen in the prologue of the first film, a mariner and the original bearer of Narya.

Boromir is seen only briefly in this *The Return of the King*, but he does get a portrait in the closing credits. Saruman and Wormtongue, who do not appear in the theatrical cut, only get portraits in the extended edition.

The credits of the extended edition contain the trilogy's last new piece of music. "Bilbo's Song," sung in Elvish by a boys' choir, is a translation of one of Bilbo's songs from the book. It's a gorgeous piece of music every fan should listen to at least once.

At the end, the score closes with an homage to Richard Wagner's *Der Ring des Nibelungen* as a pencil sketch of the Ring is shown. This is certainly fitting. The opera popularized the use of leitmotifs (themes for specific characters, places, and situations), the foundation for *The Lord of the Rings* score.

Fans celebrate at The Return of the King *Oscar Party after the film pulls off a clean sweep, winning all eleven Academy Awards it was nominated for.* (Ian Smith)

The Fellowship of the Ring and *The Two Towers* came in second at the box office in North America for 2001 and 2002, losing to the first *Harry Potter* and first *Spider-Man* films respectively. In 2004, *The Return of the King* soared past *Finding Nemo* to give *The Lord of the Rings*, in the last try, the top spot for 2003. Luck certainly played a role: had *The Return of the King* been released the year before or the year after, it would have come in second as well.

The Foolishness of a Took

The Hobbit actors had some fun with their mugs at the Green Dragon. Take a close look at the color of the mugs as the scene progresses.

In Frodo's journal, he refers to Sam's courting of Rosie as "the bravest thing he had ever done." Personally, I would have picked battling the cave-troll, entering the Tower of Cirith Ungol, or saving Frodo at Mount Doom while the whole place collapsed around them . . . but Rosie is pretty cute.

Being number one at the box office for a weekend is a huge boost for a film, giving it far greater attention and publicity than whatever is number two. So when Sony's *Big Fish* (2003) opened nationwide (in the U.S.) against *Return of the King* (then in its fourth week), Sony used a creative estimate to claim the top spot. All the other studios said Sony was mistaken, but the media still gave *Big Fish* the perks of being number one. After enjoying their film's time in the spotlight, Sony revised their figures, quietly giving the top spot back to *The Return of the King*. The next weekend both films were legitimately outgrossed by *Along Came Polly* (2004).

The Return of the King Easter Egg Alert

There is a second hidden bonus feature included with *The Return of the King* Platinum Series Special Extended Edition. On the second disc, there is an MTV spoof interview involving Ben Stiller, Vince Vaughn, and Peter Jackson. To access it, go to the "Select a Scene" menu, and once there navigate to the final group of scenes. Then navigate down at Scene 78 to reveal a hidden Ring symbol, and press "Enter."

Frequently Asked Questions

Before December 2001, my knowledge of Tolkien and the films did not mean much to most people. But when *The Fellowship of the Ring* turned *The Lord of the Rings* into the coolest bit of pop culture there was (at least for a while), I was inundated with questions from friends, family, and new fans. Here I have attempted to answer the most frequently asked questions.

What happens to the Fellowship after the events in the books and films?

Aragorn and Arwen shape Minas Tirith into a more beautiful and splendid city than ever before. They rule for 120 years in "great glory and bliss" before Aragorn hands off the scepter to his son, Eldarion. Afterward, Aragorn says to Arwen, "At last, Lady Evenstar, fairest in the world, most beloved, my world is fading." And he dies as we see in *The Two Towers*. Arwen returns to abandoned Lothlórien to die of grief.

Samwise, elected mayor of Hobbiton seven times, enjoys many years with Rosie and their thirteen children. After Rosie dies of old age, Sam sets sail from the Grey Havens to join Frodo.

Merry and Pippin also raise families and enjoy the peaceful Hobbiton life until Sam leaves. Then they journey to Rohan, where Merry says goodbye to King Éomer on the king's deathbed. From there, Merry and Pippin return to Minas Tirith where they spend the remainder of their years.

Gimli sets up a Dwarven colony in the Glittering Caves, which you can see in *The Two Towers* behind Helm's Deep. He and his people craft great works for Gondor and Rohan. After Aragorn, Merry, and Pippin have died, Gimli and Legolas also set sail for the West, and with that, the Fellowship departs Middle-earth.

How do you pronounce Tolkien?

Tol-keen (equal stress on both syllables)

Why was Burger King promoting *The Fellowship of the Ring*?

New Line Cinema had an isolated contract with Burger King that ran from November 19 to December 16, 2001. The studio was concerned at that time with building name recognition for *The Lord of the Rings*, and fast-food restaurants have gigantic advertising budgets that allow them to run many commercials every day. In 2002, New Line teamed up with Kia, an automotive company, to cross promote the first film's DVD with Sorento sport utility vehicles. The same year, the studio signed a multimillion-dollar, two-year deal with Verizon Wireless to promote *The Two Towers* and *The Return of the King*. (Somehow I don't think Tolkien had fast food, cars, and cell phones in mind when he wrote his books!)

How does Gandalf get his hat and staff back from Saruman?

He doesn't. Gandalf leaves his hat with his horse when he visits Saruman, and he carries three different staffs throughout the course of the films. The first staff is kind of a sapling with a bulbous root head that holds his pipe. The second staff has a differently shaped head, perfect for holding a magically lit stone in Moria. He loses it in the battle with the Balrog. The third staff, which is a gift from Galadriel, is white and more finely crafted. He carries this as Gandalf the White — until it's broken in the extended edition of the third film.

Why does my extended edition DVD freeze for a moment on the Fellowship's gear just before Galadriel approaches her Mirror?

The extended editions are "double-layer" DVD sets. These DVDs must have a code at some point that tells the player it's time to switch layers. Because the picture sometimes freezes momentarily during the change, DVD manufacturers try to put the code in unobtrusive places. If you watch carefully, you might be able to spot the switch about halfway through each extended edition disc.

Throughout the trilogy dead horses are shown lying on battlefields. Where did the filmmakers get these carcasses from?

The filmmakers constructed these props out of fiberglass.

In *The Two Towers* preview (included as an Easter egg on *The Fellowship of the Ring* DVD) there is footage of Éowyn hiding from an Orc. When does this take place?

This was to take place during the Helm's Deep battle. A group of Orcs slip into the caves only to be cut down by Éowyn, demonstrating her "skill with the blade." Curiously, this was the second time these filmmakers tried something like this only to find it was anticlimactic. When Wood and Astin were first shot in the boat together for the end of *The Fellowship of the Ring*, an Orc was filmed rising out of the water, trying to pull Frodo under.

Aragorn uses a *palantír* at Minas Tirith in the extended edition of *The Return of the King*. How does he take the palantír with him on the Paths of the Dead? Or is it Denethor's *palantír* that he uses?

Denethor does not have a *palantír* in this film adaptation. Actually, Gandalf takes Saruman's *palantír* to Minas Tirith. Watch carefully as he prepares to set off with Pippin, and you'll see it, still covered, in his hand. The cover remains until Aragorn removes it.

What if Frodo had killed Gollum at Mount Doom and kept the Ring? Could he overthrow Sauron?

No. According to Tolkien, the Nazgûl would attempt to remove Frodo from Sammath Naur and destroy the entrance. Sauron would then take the Ring from Frodo.

Toward the end of the credits in all three films are a few lines in a strange language. Is this Elvish?

No, the lines are Te Reo Maori. The project began and ended with blessings from the Maori, the indigenous Polynesian people of New Zealand. The translations are:

> First film: "*We would like to acknowledge the people of New Zealand. May God from above care for you in the New Year.*"

> Second film: "*Peace on earth, Goodwill to all mankind.*"

> Third film: "*Let us dedicate our memories to the spirits of the Eldar who came to us from the Ocean that lies to the West.*"

The filmmakers made some mistakes, proving they are human. Did Tolkien make any goofs?

Yes. There are several in the book, including my personal favorite, when Gimli claims at Helm's Deep that he hasn't killed any Orcs since Moria. Apparently, the battle at Amon Hen slipped Tolkien's mind. The Dwarf certainly would remember! That said, both Tolkien and the filmmakers did a marvelous job with their creations. Hopefully, if I made any mistakes with this book, my readers will understand that like all of us, I can only do my best and hope it's enough.

Is *The Lord of the Rings* one film or three?

Some point out that the films were written and shot concurrently and believe this makes them one large picture. However, scriptwriting and principal photography are only part of the filmmaking process, and the postproduction for each film was handled individually (each film even had its own editor). Also, Jackson wished for each of the films to feel different. *The Fellowship of the Ring* is the fantasy film with an exotic feel. *The Two Towers* is gritty and muddy with a theme of hopelessness. *The Return of the King* is epic and majestic with a feeling of hope reborn. That's not to say they can't be connected into one larger adventure. Perhaps the best way to look at it is that it's one story, told through three acts.

Q&A
with Design Artist Daniel Falconer

As a longtime fan of both J.R.R. Tolkien and illustration, conceptual work for *The Lord of the Rings* films was a dream job for Daniel Falconer. This New Zealander was intimately involved in the design of creatures, armor, weaponry, props, and costuming for the trilogy. On February 23, 2005, shortly after the release of *The Return of the King* extended edition, he answered some of my questions.

Braun: How did you become interested in *The Lord of the Rings*?

Falconer: My mother gave me a much-loved and thumbed through copy of *The Lord of the Rings* in one paperback volume when I was eleven. Many of the pages were falling out, but I protected that book like it was my own flesh. I was so thoroughly enthralled by it that I devoured it in no time at all and then kept going back for more — rereading favorite parts all through my teenage years. I loved every page that Gollum was on — the dynamic between the two Hobbits and him was just so much fun to read and imagine. I also loved the Ents because they were so magical, and reading their scenes conjured up strong imagery in my head.

Braun: How did you become interested in illustration and design?

Falconer: Being the child of an art teacher, I was encouraged to explore art throughout my childhood. I maintain that more folks can draw than they realize. The problem is that we are so often discouraged when young, lose confidence, and consequently never draw again. I am thankful that my mother encouraged and supported my creativity. She actively fostered it, and kept me well stocked with art materials of all kinds, from paints and felt pens to polystyrene and cardboard packaging that I would reshape into environments for my toys. We had Plasticene and clay as kids, and would make our own fun. That basis of confidence in one's own artistic ability, coupled with an insatiable desire to be making and creating things, set me up to be able to pursue this as a career path. I had known ever since I saw such movies as *Star Wars* and *The Dark Crystal* that I wanted to end up in the film industry. It wasn't so much that I wanted to make films as I wanted to create new worlds and tell stories in them. After seeing "making of" documentaries about films like those I mentioned, I realized that you could actually do that for a living. From that point on, I knew it's what I wanted to do, and all my schooling and university education became geared toward achieving that goal.

Braun: What did it mean to you when you found out you'd be working on *The Lord of the Rings*?

Falconer: Being a longtime fan, I had always hoped to one day be involved in bringing it to the big screen as a live-action endeavor. In my wildest dreams, I never expected to find myself working at the place that would be handed the project to make — especially so early in my career. I had only been at Weta a year when it came along — that's one year out of art school and here I am designing the greatest fantasy novel of all time as three huge-budget movies! No pressure!

The level of excitement I felt was fever-pitched, but because of the secrecy agreements I had signed, and the desire by the studio to keep the project under wraps, I couldn't tell anyone what I was doing. Even my family didn't know what we were working on, only that it was going to be big. The joy I felt when the project was green-lit and we could talk about it was immense. It was an exhausted high that lasted over six years.

Braun: What did you like doing most?

Falconer: I think to pick a favorite, it would be designing and building Treebeard and the Ents, just because I was afforded great freedom to realize them in a way that most married with my own creative vision of them from the books. There is also something very cool about a real physical creature. We built Treebeard as a giant puppet, and it was just so cool to be able to be involved with that. Standing next to that puppet on set was a thrill.

Braun: Did you know what you wanted right away with the Ents, or did the design take a while?

Falconer: I had a strong vision of the Ents after reading the books, so in one sense, that was easy to get down on paper for me, but, as with any design, there are always issues to resolve in the design that don't show themselves until you draw them.

For that, the process in which the designs are honed and improved is invaluable. It helps sort out any problems with the design, and gives you the chance to improve it, tweaking little things here and there to get the best possible result. The

Ents were established with the very first drawings done, but they had to be honed and developed to really work. That came about with everyone's input. It was also important to come up with other options, even if they were discarded, just to be sure that we had indeed settled on the right choice.

Braun: How did your knowledge of the books help you on the project?
Falconer: I actually ended up becoming one of the "go-to" guys for Tolkien knowledge. I remember with great fondness the day we were all in the Weta cinema watching rushes (the results of the day's shooting) and a debate was being had between some of the department heads as to some creative issue. Peter Jackson called out in the dark room, asking if I was there. He wanted to know what Tolkien had to say about it, and thought I was the man to know the answer. That was a very proud moment for me, and one that made all those years of being a nerd at school worthwhile. At last that knowledge gleaned with my head in a book while others were out playing sports had born fruit in the end!

Once shooting started, I was also asked to provide handout folders for some of the cast who hadn't had the time to read the books before beginning work. I prepared detailed folders for several of the main cast, particularly the Elves, with family trees, relevant sections from the books, character bios, and personality insights. I got to sit with several of them and talk about their characters, sometimes on multiple occasions.

Braun: And you even got to be an Elf yourself at Helm's Deep.
Falconer: I was lucky with Helm's Deep. I was only there a couple of times, and mostly that was shooting indoors during the day. Most of Helm's Deep was shot on location at night. It played havoc with crew sanity because it was a long, hard, cold, wet, dark shoot. I think I got very lucky in getting to dodge all that hard work.

Braun: What happened to all you Elves at Helm's Deep? Did you all die?
Falconer: It was never explicitly stated that all the Elves died, but after the battle, you can't see any left standing, leading one to wonder, "Did they all get pasted?" In a romantic sense, the idea that they all gave their immortal lives in a sacrifice to buy time for Rohan is a wonderful one, and I think perhaps one that Tolkien might have approved of. The final answer though, as to whether any survived at all, will probably never be known. I think if any had, they would have been quick to leave for their homes and the sanctity that they had amid such carnage. I doubt any Elf who survived that would be left with much taste for lingering in Middle-earth.

Braun: Did you get to do a cameo for the third film?

Falconer: I did try, but it fell through. There was talk of the Design Department getting to be Dead Men of Dunharrow, but it never happened.

Braun: For those of you who had been longtime fans of the books, how did you deal with having different visions of how things should look?

Falconer: As a concept artist you are always balancing several creative agendas. When designing something for *The Lord of the Rings*, you are trying to realize Peter Jackson's vision, stay true to Tolkien's vision, create something fans will like, and also satisfy your own creative vision. Fortunately we usually got several cracks at it, sometimes submitting hundreds of drawings before the final design was approved. That gave us the chance to get our own feelings down on paper and also hone in on what Peter Jackson wanted. It also meant that all the options were thoroughly explored. We couldn't be unhappy with the final result if it didn't match our own personal vision exactly, because we had plenty of opportunities to present our own ideas. In the end, the best ideas rose to the top of the pile and stood out, but all options were considered. Accepting that sometimes an idea one might really like doesn't make it through is part of the job. It doesn't pay to get too attached to a concept. It's important to remain objective.

Braun: What do you think of the films as a whole?

Falconer: They are my favorite films. I love them. Fortunately the project was so large that, even having worked on them since the very beginning, there was still huge amounts that I never saw till the cinema release, so I could appreciate them as a fan and not just as a crew member.

Braun: As a fan of both Tolkien and special edition DVDs, I love the Platinum Series Special Editions. Michael Pellerin and his people seem to have poured so much work into them. What was it like working with them?

Falconer: I cannot speak highly enough of Michael Pellerin, Susie Lee, and the rest of the DVD team. These guys have become great friends of ours through the production. They were intimately involved with all aspects of the films throughout the whole job. They knew us all well and were keen to do right by us — telling the full story of these amazing movies. We did several interviews with them, and also looked through our artwork with them. Bottom line though, the DVDs are as good as they are because Michael and Susie know us all so well, and know all the stories. They know what to dig for to make great content on the DVDs and they are phenomenally talented, smart people. I'm really glad you asked that question because these guys often get forgotten, yet they are as important in the equation as any of us.

Braun: Okay, now to the tough questions. I'm going to list some choices, and I want you to select your preference. Best Peter Jackson cameo: man of Bree, spear-thrower at Helm's Deep, or mercenary of the Anduin?
Falconer: Mercenary without a doubt. How cool was that scene in the extended edition of *Return of the King*?

Braun: Best Peter Jackson kids cameo: cute Hobbit children, cute Rohan refugees, or cute Gondor kids?
Falconer: Hobbit kids — just too cute for words, especially their reactions to Bilbo's story.

Braun: Line most likely to have Tolkien rolling over in his grave: "Nobody tosses a Dwarf," "Meat's back on the menu, boys!," "It's the Dwarves that go swimming with little, hairy women."
Falconer: Tie between the first two. There were those moments that made even some of us wince with awareness that we were perhaps treading a little close to the edge. . . .

Braun: Sexier babe: Éowyn or Arwen?
Falconer: Tough call. I'm going to pass on the grounds that my wife might read this.

Braun: Better singer: Éowyn or Arwen?
Falconer: Both great — but I cried for Éowyn's lament.

Braun: Character you'd least like to kiss: Lurtz or the Mouth of Sauron?
Falconer: The Watcher in the Water — just ewwwwww!

Braun: *Lord of the Rings* the books or *Lord of the Rings* the movies?
Falconer: As much as I love the films, if they only serve as an eleven hour–long advertisement for the books, then that's fine by me. Go read them everyone! No contest for the power of the written word. The films just make them more accessible for many who might otherwise never have read them.

Braun: Bakshi's *Lord of the Rings* or the Rankin/Bass *Return of the King?*
Falconer: Never seen the Rankin/Bass movie, but I really loved parts of Bakshi's

labor of love. The guy really got some things right, and did a great job with the technology he had. It's easy to be critical in the wake of the live-action films, but when you consider the difference in tech, budget, and support, Bakshi deserves some serious credit. His film enriched my experience of the books in the same way I hope ours will for future readers. You watch them, take what you like onboard and disregard the rest in favor of your own imagination as inspired by the books.

Braun: Better idea: *The Hobbit* the movie or *The Hobbit* the miniseries?
Falconer: The movie, in my opinion — just because I doubt that a miniseries would have the budget that *The Hobbit* deserves, and the Battle of Five Armies demands to be seen on the big screen.

Braun: Furthest from an Oscar caliber performance: artist Christian Rivers as the beacon keeper, composer Howard Shore as a happy Man of Rohan, or producer Rick Porras as the frightened pirate when the Army of the Dead attack his ship?
Falconer: Ha! I should say Rivers because he's a good friend, and I'd hate to pass up the chance to rib him. Actually, I thought he was great. My prize goes to the Uruk-hai tiptoeing down the steps at Amon Hen.

Braun: Sounds more like a lecturing college professor in the DVD bonus features: Richard Taylor or Alex Funke?
Falconer: Oh poor Richard — he actually sounds quite different in person. I think he intentionally speaks very clearly and slowly on the DVDs to be sure he gets his point across. He is a very good public speaker and is intensely passionate about what he saying. I think it's important to remember that he has told these stories thousands of times, so that probably affects the telling. Go easy on him — he's one of the most amazing people you'll ever meet!

Braun: Favorite film: *The Fellowship of the Ring*, *The Two Towers*, or *The Return of the King*?
Falconer: *Return of the King* because it has the emotional payoff. It is also the end of the journey, for us as well as the characters, so it has added emotional weight. I haven't yet managed to watch it without getting choked up in places.

Braun: What has it been like to have worked on a project so big for so long? Does it seem a bit anticlimactic to move on to something else?
Falconer: It's hard to imagine what could top *The Lord of the Rings*, but every new project has its own challenges and joys. I will always remember what *The Lord of*

the Rings was to me, and what an incredible time it was in my life. It has changed me deeply, and I am hugely thankful to the project and Tolkien for how my life has been enriched by *The Lord of the Rings*, both professionally and creatively.

Braun: Do you have anything you'd like to say to the fans?

Falconer: I think what we have about covers it, but I'll say a big thank-you to all those fans I have had the pleasure of meeting. I am constantly amazed by how generous, articulate, and warm the fans are. It's a wonderful community to be a part of, and I have been lucky enough to meet some incredible people and hear some amazing stories. I have made many lasting friendships as a result.

Recurring Themes Toteboard

("EE" denotes Extended Edition only)

Number of times Frodo falls down — 38

- When firework Smaug flies overhead
- When Pippin knocks him over in Farmer Maggot's field
- Soon after, when all four Hobbits tumble down the slope
- After he jumps onto the ferry
- At the Prancing Pony, when trying to stop Pippin from talking
- Seconds after the first fall at the Prancing Pony (he stands up and falls down again)
- As Aragorn tosses him into one of the Prancing Pony guestrooms
- As he attempts to run from the Nazgûl at Amon Sûl
- While climbing Caradhras
- When he's snatched by the Watcher in the Water
- After the cave-troll spears him
- After he sees the Eye of Sauron in Galadriel's Mirror
- As Boromir trips him during their argument
- As the Fellowship fights Orcs at Amon Hen
- As he takes the Ring off after looking out from the high seat of Amon Hen
- When shoved by Gollum during their first fight
- Shoved down by Gollum again
- At the Dead Marshes . . . kerplunk!
- When Gollum pulls him backward at the Black Gate
- When Faramir shoves him down at their first meeting
- When Sam pushes him down the stairs at Osgiliath
- As the ground shakes just before Minas Morgul sends a signal
- After he stops Sam from hitting Gollum
- As he's scrambling in Shelob's lair before meeting the spider

- ○ Seconds later (he stands up and falls down again)
- ○ As Shelob first attacks
- ○ Again, seconds later
- ○ Just after telling Gollum he must destroy the Ring
- ○ Just after telling the absent Sam he's so sorry
- ○ As he's stung by Shelob
- ○ When Sam hits him in Mordor to escape the Orcs (EE)
- ○ Just before Sam decides to throw their gear away (EE)
- ○ When Sauron's Eye almost finds him in Mordor
- ○ While ascending Mount Doom
- ○ When Gollum first attacks at Mount Doom
- ○ When Gollum takes the Ring
- ○ As Frodo and Gollum struggle for the Ring
- ○ As Mount Doom erupts
- ○ As he boards the ship at the Grey Havens

(Okay, the last one isn't true, but I'm surprised at that)

Number of times Sam eavesdrops — 7

- ○ At Bag End when Frodo and Gandalf are talking
- ○ On the road when the Wood-Elves pass by (EE)
- ○ At the Council of Elrond
- ○ At the Black Gate
- ○ As the Southrons pass by and are attacked
- ○ As Gollum and Sméagol plot murder
- ○ As the Orcs find Frodo's stung body

Number of times Aragorn tosses somebody — 3

- ○ He tosses Frodo at the Prancing Pony
- ○ He tosses Sam at Moria
- ○ He tosses Gimli at Helm's Deep

(I think he would toss Merry if the hobbit were to be in his way after the Beacons of Gondor are lit)

Number of times the writers play the old "He's dead! No wait, he isn't really" trick — 17

- ○ With the Hobbits at the Prancing Pony when the Nazgûl appear to stab them
- ○ With the Nazgûl at the Ford of Bruinen when they are taken by the river

- With Frodo at the Ford of Rivendell as he drifts into a white light
- With Frodo when the cave-troll spears him
- With Gandalf at Moria
- With the Orc who looks up as Aragorn runs over to a dying Boromir
- With Pippin as he appears to be stomped by a horse
- With Grishnákh who appears to be killed by the Riders of Rohan
- With Aragorn as he falls over a cliff
- With Arwen who appears to be dying and is forgotten about until the Ring is destroyed
- With Faramir after he's shot and Denethor says it's all over
- With Gollum as he falls over a cliff, doing his Aragorn impression (did Brego save him too?)
- With Frodo as he's stung by Shelob
- With Merry before he's found by Pippin
- With Éowyn discovered on the battlefield (EE)
- With Frodo as he appears to fall with Gollum into the lava
- With Frodo and Sam who appear to die as Mount Doom erupts

Number of times a Hobbit says, "What are you doing?" — 6

- Frodo when Gandalf takes the envelope and Ring and throws them in the fire
- Frodo when the Hobbits light a fire at Amon Sûl
- Sam when Aragorn lets Arwen ride away with Frodo
- Tom Riddle when Harry prepares to destroy the diary (oops, wrong movie)
- Sam when Frodo walks away from Sam at Osgiliath
- Pippin when Merry checks out their height at Orthanc (EE)
- Merry just before Pippin steals the *palantír*

Characters accused of being late — 4

- Gandalf when approaching Bag End
- Uglúk who is told his master grows impatient (EE)
- Aragorn when arriving at Helm's Deep
- The pirate scum during the Battle of the Pelennor Fields

How much "heart" these movies have — 27

- Bilbo says, "I think in his heart Frodo is still in love with the Shire."
- Bilbo says, "I may not look it, but I begin to feel it in my heart."

- Merry and Pippin sing, "To heal my heart and drown my woe." (EE)
- Aragorn says, "You have a stout heart, little Hobbit."
- Arwen says, "It is mine to give to whom I will. Like my heart."
- Elrond says, "In her heart your mother knew you'd be hunted all your life." (EE)
- Gandalf says, "My heart tells me Gollum has some part to play yet, for good or ill."
- Haldir says, "Caras Galadhon, the heart of Elvendom on Earth." (EE)
- Galadriel says, "Do not let the great emptiness of Khazad-dûm fill your heart." (EE)
- Galadriel says, "Do not let your hearts be troubled."
- Legolas says, "I have not the heart to tell you."
- Galadriel says, "I do not deny my heart has greatly desired this."
- Frodo says, "It would seem like wisdom, but for the warning in my heart."
- Gollum says, "Cold be heart and hand and bone."
- Treebeard says, "Anger festers in their hearts."
- Faramir says, "And if he was really evil at heart." (EE)
- Arwen says again, "It is mine to give to whom I will. Like my heart."
- Galadriel says, "In his heart, Frodo begins to understand . . ."
- Faramir says, "More than this I know it in my heart." (EE)
- Denethor says, "Ever the Ring will seek to corrupt the hearts of lesser men." (EE)
- Saruman says, "Something festers in the heart of Middle-earth." (EE)
- Aragorn says, "What does your heart tell you?"
- Éomer says, "I do not doubt his heart, only the reach of his arm."
- Éowyn says, "Take heart, Merry." (EE)
- Arwen sings, "With a deepening heart . . ." (EE)
- Aragorn says, "I see in your eyes the same fear that would take the heart of me!"
- Frodo says, "When in your heart, you begin to understand."

The Ring Comes Full Circle
Coming Soon: *The Hobbit* (2011, 2012)

Don't put away your wizard costume just yet! When Gandalf assures us that "the journey does not end here" in *The Return of the King*, he means it. Gandalf, Bilbo, and other old favorites will be back in theaters to kick off another decade.

Peter Jackson, serving as executive producer, and many of the people who helped him make *The Lord of the Rings*, are working on two prequel films based on Tolkien's book *The Hobbit*. The films, to be shot in New Zealand in 2010, will be directed by Guillermo del Toro, the Mexican filmmaker famous for *Hellboy* (2004) and *Pan's Labyrinth* (2006). Del Toro, selected to direct by Peter Jackson, has been a fan of *The Hobbit* for thirty years and has helped Jackson, Fran Walsh, and Philippa Boyens write the screenplays. It is their hope that all five of their Middle-earth films will connect with each other, with the tone progressing from light to dark as we follow the story from *The Hobbit* to *The Return of the King*.

Many of the old gang are getting back together. Howard Shore will compose the films' scores, and Weta will again be bringing Middle-earth to life. McKellen and Serkis will reprise the roles of Gandalf and Gollum, and other actors from *The Lord of the Rings* have expressed interest in returning to their roles as well.

The films will be released around Christmas in 2011 and 2012, exactly ten years after the debut of *The Fellowship of the Ring* and *The Two Towers*. Bilbo says he's quite ready for another adventure. Are you?

Activity Section
(More Fun than a Bombadil Run)

Movie Trivia
Some might call it trivial, but I'm a trivia purist. If these questions cause you to cry out "What does it matter?!" then I've done my job. Circle your choice. The answers can be found on page 209.

1. **According to Galadriel, how many years does the Ring lay in the Anduin River?**
   a. 2500 years
   b. 3000 years
   c. 3500 years

2. **What words follow the title screen in the theatrical cut of *The Fellowship of the Ring*?**
   a. "60 years later . . . The Shire"
   b. "The Shire . . . 60 years later"
   c. "60 years later in the Shire"

3. **What flavor jam does Bilbo have?**
   a. Apricot
   b. Apple
   c. Raspberry

4. **Which Hobbit from the books does Bilbo shake hands with at the long expected party?**
   a. Rory Brandybuck
   b. Fatty Bolger
   c. Odo Proudfoot

5. **Where do the Bracegirdles come from?**
   a. Hardbottle
   b. Bywater
   c. Frogmorten

6. **What year did Isildur make the scroll Gandalf discovers?**
   a. 4343 First Age
   b. 3434 Second Age
   c. 3443 Third Age

7. **What is the first thing Arwen says to Frodo?**
   a. "Frodo"
   b. "*Lasto beth nin*"
   c. "*Telin le thaed*"

8. **What time does Frodo wake up at Rivendell?**
   a. Nine in the morning
   b. Ten in the morning
   c. Eleven in the morning

9. **When the Crebain from Dunland fly over the Fellowship, who puts out the cooking fire?**
   a. Sam
   b. Frodo
   c. Merry

10. **What is the last spoken word in *The Fellowship of the Ring*?**
    a. You
    b. Sam
    c. Me

11. **What phase is the Moon in when Frodo and Sam first meet Gollum?**
    a. Full
    b. Waning Crescent
    c. Waxing Crescent

12. **According to Saruman, where did the Rohirrim drive the Wild Men?**
   a. The forests
   b. The hills
   c. The wild

13. **What is the only food the Orcs have to eat when they hold Merry and Pippin captive?**
   a. Bread
   b. Man flesh
   c. Moldy meat

14. **How old does Legolas say Fangorn is?**
   a. Very Old
   b. Ancient
   c. Ageless

15. **Where does Treebeard say his home is?**
   a. In the northern part of the forest
   b. Near the roots of the mountain
   c. He doesn't say

16. **How many arrows does Legolas fire in slow motion at the Orcs and Wargs before mounting his horse?**
   a. One
   b. Two
   c. Three

17. **What does the Gondorian Ranger whisper into Faramir's ear just before Faramir takes Frodo and Sam to the Forbidden Pool?**
   a. "We found the third one."
   b. "The creature is here."
   c. "The scouts say there's a hot babe at Helm's Deep."

18. **When Aragorn arrives at Helm's Deep, what does Gimli say he's going to do?**
   a. Burst with joy
   b. Hug Aragorn
   c. Kill Aragorn

19. **What does Théoden say he wishes Rohan's end to be?**
    a. Worthy of a song
    b. Worthy of a tale
    c. Worthy of remembrance

20. **Which does Aragorn claim stands ready to defend Helm's Deep instead of soldiers?**
    a. Farmers, riders, and faeries
    b. Stable boys, faeries, and farmers
    c. Farmers, farriers, and stable boys

21. **Whose lap does Pippin kick a tankard into while singing with Merry at Edoras?**
    a. Grimbold
    b. Gamling
    c. Éothain

22. **What does Gandalf say to Shadowfax in the third film when it's time to race to Minas Tirith?**
    a. "Show us the meaning of haste"
    b. "Ride like the wind, Shadowfax."
    c. "On, Shadowfax!"

23. **Which beacon is mentioned by name in these films?**
    a. Min-Rimmon
    b. Amon Dîn
    c. Nardol

24. **After Théoden says, "Rohan will answer," how many times do we hear the Rohan warning bell clang?**
    a. Four
    b. Five
    c. Seven

25. **Where does Grimbold come from?**
    a. The Westfold
    b. Fenmarch
    c. Snowbourne

26. **To whom does Legolas say the Dead Men swore an oath?**
    a. The first King of Gondor
    b. The last King of Gondor
    c. The Kings of Gondor

27. **When Théoden is organizing the Rohirrim for the Battle of the Pelennor Fields, where does he tell Gamling to take his *éored*?**
    a. To the left
    b. Down the center
    c. To the right

28. **When Sam is attacking the Orcs at the Tower of Cirith Ungol, to whom does he dedicate the second swing of his sword?**
    a. His old Gaffer
    b. Frodo
    c. The Shire

29. **When the Hobbits stand before Aragorn and Arwen, which of the four is the last to bow?**
    a. Merry
    b. Pippin
    c. Sam

30. **In what order does Frodo say goodbye to his friends?**
    a. Merry, Pippin, Sam
    b. Pippin, Merry, Sam
    c. Pippin, Sam, Merry

Crossword Puzzle

Across

1. King of Gondor
4. The London school where Sean Bean learned the craft of acting
6. Two of these were featured in the second movie
7. Sam might have another one of these
8. The number of Nazgûl
10. Arwen's symbol of immortality
13. A village where Peter Jackson has a cameo
14. An Elvish forest
17. You'll get a list of millions of sites at this search engine if you type in "Orlando Bloom"
18. The Ring was this to Isildur
20. Wormtongue claims Éomer does this
21. Sam wonders if he and Frodo will ever be put into these

Down

1. A Fellowship actor
2. Aragorn's true love
3. Sam's true love
4. The horse masters' country
5. Elves and Men formed one of these
9. Cate Blanchett was lit with a special one of these
11. Hobbits and Elves can be identified in part by these enlarged body parts
12. The Lord of the Rings
13. Aragorn's horse
15. Gandalf the Grey's middle name
16. Number of Fellowship members
19. Figwit is one

(Answers on page 209)

Fan or Nonfan?

The Lord of the Rings was an interesting film project, with fans and non-fans combining their talents to create movies that everyone could enjoy.

By circling correctly "fan" or "nonfan," see if you can identify which actors were fans of the book before taking their parts and which were not (answers on page 210).

1. Sir Ian McKellen (Gandalf):   **FAN** **NONFAN**

2. Sir Ian Holm (Bilbo):   **FAN** **NONFAN**

3. Sean Astin (Sam):   **FAN** **NONFAN**

4. Andy Serkis (Gollum):   **FAN** **NONFAN**

5. Bernard Hill (Théoden):   **FAN** **NONFAN**

6. Bruce Hopkins (Gamling):   **FAN** **NONFAN**

7. Miranda Otto (Éowyn):   **FAN** **NONFAN**

8. Karl Urban (Éomer):   **FAN** **NONFAN**

9. Viggo Mortensen (Aragorn):   **FAN** **NONFAN**

10. Sean Bean (Boromir):   **FAN** **NONFAN**

11. Billy Boyd (Pippin):   **FAN** **NONFAN**

12. Dominic Monaghan (Merry):   **FAN** **NONFAN**

13. Craig Parker (Haldir):   **FAN** **NONFAN**

14. Liv Tyler (Arwen):   **FAN** **NONFAN**

15. Orlando Bloom (Legolas)   **FAN** **NONFAN**

Word Search

See if you can find the listed names in the main puzzle below. The names do not need to be in a straight line, but can snake around the puzzle up, down, right, left, and diagonally, so long as no letter is used twice in the same name and all letters are next to each other. For example, Frodo can be found in the sample puzzle below:

```
F  G  X  S
P  R  O  B
M  T  D  O
```

Names: **Frodo, Gandalf, Aragorn, Arwen, Figwit, Haldir, Lurtz, Treebeard, Bilbo, Faramir, Sauron, Saruman, Gothmog, Legolas, Denethor**

```
S  R  O  S  A  R  T  W  R  B  Z  X  N  F  U  R
A  U  O  F  R  U  E  E  A  N  I  R  O  S  L  T
M  A  R  A  A  R  Q  S  M  E  E  L  L  R  Z  M
L  E  G  I  M  O  M  U  A  R  U  R  O  G  A  I
D  X  T  R  U  L  U  R  T  S  M  E  B  R  F  M
E  E  H  A  K  R  F  A  S  D  A  H  O  M  R  R
N  D  O  P  O  E  L  L  F  D  D  P  P  A  R  K
H  H  Z  E  A  D  G  O  R  F  P  I  D  L  A  H
T  R  W  A  N  A  D  T  M  G  O  P  O  Z  S  S
Q  V  R  X  R  Q  A  H  O  T  H  T  H  G  T  C
B  R  A  U  N  W  D  E  V  Y  D  Y  E  M  O  F
D  U  M  F  K  D  E  T  B  K  N  I  M  O  Y  K
L  O  N  W  Y  G  R  R  E  I  O  V  I  E  Y  E
R  A  S  A  N  A  N  A  K  B  L  H  D  Y  L  E
O  U  I  G  D  O  D  R  F  W  J  Y  J  G  N  J
Z  W  L  A  O  R  Z  Z  E  T  B  U  A  O  R  D
Y  T  G  I  F  I  D  L  N  E  H  B  U  R  A  N
L  A  I  W  G  H  A  Z  Z  D  O  R  F  L  A  G
```

Film or Book Invention?

Jackson once commented that during the course of his project his mind became a bit muddled, and it became difficult for him to separate what was originally Tolkien's idea and what was his. Now is your chance to test your knowledge on the matter. Below are items, events, and ideas found in the films. Attempt to correctly identify whether they were originally an invention of Tolkien (**BOOK**) or the scriptwriters (**FILM**), and circle your answer for each. (The answers are on page 212.)

1. Pippin attends Bilbo's birthday party   **BOOK**   **FILM**
2. The One Ring is inscripted on the inside and outside   **BOOK**   **FILM**
3. The entrance to Orthanc faces the gate of Isengard   **BOOK**   **FILM**
4. Frodo is stabbed at Amon Sûl   **BOOK**   **FILM**
5. Elrond, at Mount Doom, tells Isildur he should destroy the Ring   **BOOK**   **FILM**
6. The Grand Chamber of Rivendell   **BOOK**   **FILM**
7. The Evenstar pendant   **BOOK**   **FILM**
8. The blond hair of Legolas   **BOOK**   **FILM**
9. A full Moon illuminates the Doors of Moria for the Fellowship   **BOOK**   **FILM**
10. Pippin throws a stone into the water by the Doors   **BOOK**   **FILM**
11. The Doors of Moria that the Fellowship enter open outward   **BOOK**   **FILM**
12. Gandalf tells Frodo, "All we have to decide is what to do with the time that is given us."   **BOOK**   **FILM**
13. Lady Galadriel gives Legolas a bow of the Galadhrim (extended edition)   **BOOK**   **FILM**
14. Gríma Wormtongue's thuggish friends at Rohan   **BOOK**   **FILM**
15. The Orc-head on a stake left by the Riders of Rohan   **BOOK**   **FILM**
16. Éothain and Freda, children of Rohan   **BOOK**   **FILM**
17. The Ring of Barahir   **BOOK**   **FILM**
18. The entrance to the Glittering Caves of Aglarond is at Helm's Deep   **BOOK**   **FILM**
19. The Helm's Deep fortress has a secret side door   **BOOK**   **FILM**
20. Denethor asks Boromir to bring him a mighty gift (extended edition)   **BOOK**   **FILM**

21. Frodo and Sam wonder if they will be put into tales   **BOOK**   **FILM**
22. The Beacons of Gondor speed their fire westward as a call for aid   **BOOK**   **FILM**
23. Gandalf zaps the Nazgûl with a white light   **BOOK**   **FILM**
24. Denethor asks Pippin to sing a song   **BOOK**   **FILM**
25. Gothmog, lieutenant and second in command to the Lord of the Nazgûl   **BOOK**   **FILM**
26. The Orcs fling heads into the city of Minas Tirith   **BOOK**   **FILM**
27. Aragorn's horse will not enter the Paths of the Dead   **BOOK**   **FILM**
28. Denethor dives off the pier of rock to his death   **BOOK**   **FILM**
29. Théoden and Aragorn arrive at Minas Tirith the same day   **BOOK**   **FILM**
30. Théoden says goodbye to Éowyn on his deathbed   **BOOK**   **FILM**
31. At Minas Tirith, Aragorn tells the Army of the Dead its oath is fulfilled   **BOOK**   **FILM**

Aragorn's Ring of Barahir. (Tom Wuellette)

Birthdays

Birthday	Name	Importance
January 3	J.R.R. Tolkien	Author
January 13	Orlando Bloom	"Legolas"
January 27	Cliff Broadway	*Ringers* Writer
January 28	Elijah Wood	"Frodo"
February 11	Paul Norell	"King of the Dead"
February 25	Sean Astin	"Sam"
February 28	Mark Ferguson	"Gil-galad"
February 28	Saul Zaentz	Copyright holder
March 18	Brad Dourif	"Wormtongue"
March 20	Lawrence Makoare	"Lurtz," "Gothmog"
April 4	Hugo Weaving	"Elrond"
April 17	Sean Bean	"Boromir"
April 20	Andy Serkis	"Gollum"
April 22	Mark Ordesky	Producer
May 5	John Rhys-Davies	"Gimli"
May 14	Cate Blanchett	"Galadriel"
May 16	Emilíana Torrini	Singer
May 17	Enya	Singer

Birthday	Name	Importance
May 25	Sir Ian McKellen	"Gandalf"
May 27	Sir Christopher Lee	"Saruman"
May 30	Todd Rippon	"Harad leader"
June 7	Karl Urban	"Éomer"
June 29	Bret McKenzie	"Figwit"
June 30	Marton Csokas	"Celeborn"
July 1	Liv Tyler	"Arwen"
July 2	J.W. Braun	Author
July 8	Fran Walsh	Writer
July 14	Brian Sibley	BBC radio writer
July 16	Calum Gittins	"Haleth"
July 18	Sarah McLeod	"Rosie"
July 18	Xoanon	TheOneRing.net founder
August 1	Cameron Rhodes	"Farmer Maggot"
August 5	Alan Howard	"One Ring" (voice)
August 16	Jasmine Watson	Jeweler
August 20	John Noble	"Denethor"
August 20	Alan Lee	Artist
August 21	John Howe	Artist

Birthday	Name	Importance
August 28	Billy Boyd	"Pippin"
September 12	Sir Ian Holm	"Bilbo"
September 13	Bruce Phillips	"Grimbold"
September 17	Bruce Spence	"Mouth of Sauron"
September 21	David Wenham	"Faramir"
September 22	Sala Baker	"Sauron"
September 28	Kiran Shah	Scale double
October 12	Alex Funke	Supervisor of miniatures
October 18	Howard Shore	Composer
October 20	Viggo Mortensen	"Aragorn"
October 31	Peter Jackson	Director
November 12	Craig Parker	"Haldir"
November 25	Bruce Hopkins	"Gamling"
November 27	Alexandra Astin	"Elanor"
December 8	Dominic Monaghan	"Merry"
December 16	Miranda Otto	"Éowyn"
December 17	Bernard Hill	"Théoden"
December 25	Annie Lennox	Singer
December 29	Brian Sergent	"Ted Sandyman"

Answers

Movie Trivia

1.	a		16.	b
2.	b		17.	a
3.	c		18.	c
4.	b		19.	c
5.	a		20.	c
6.	b		21.	b
7.	a		22.	a
8.	b		23.	b
9.	a		24.	c
10.	c		25.	a
11.	c		26.	b
12.	b		27.	b
13.	a		28.	c
14.	a		29.	a
15.	b		30.	a

If your total score is:

1–10 correct: Gandalf might say you were inattentive.

11–20 correct: Like Gimli, your eyes and ears could use some sharpening.

21–30 correct: Your attention to detail rivals Aragorn's!

Crossword Puzzle

Across

1. Aragorn

4. RADA (Royal Academy of Dramatic Art)

6. Towers

7. Ale
8. Nine
10. Evenstar
13. Bree
14. Lothlórien
17. Google
18. Bane
20. Lie
21. Tales

Down

1. Astin
2. Arwen
3. Rosie
4. Rohan
5. Alliance
9. Eyelight
11. Earlobes
12. Sauron
13. Brego
15. The
16. Nine
19. Elf

Fan or Nonfan?

1. **Sir Ian McKellen:** *Nonfan.* Being that he's from England, and that he became such a fan of the books, it's tempting to think of McKellen as a longtime fan, yet he never read them until taking the part of Gandalf.

2. **Sir Ian Holm:** *Fan.* Holm voiced Frodo in the 1981 BBC radio adaptation.

3. **Sean Astin:** *Nonfan.* Astin didn't know Bilbo from Frodo when his agent told him about the project. He was a fan of Jackson and Walsh.

4. **Andy Serkis:** *Nonfan.* Serkis read *The Hobbit*, but he never got around to *The Lord of the Rings* until becoming involved with the film project. He

was surprised (and pleased) to see Gollum's role was greater than he expected.

5. **Bernard Hill:** *Fan.* Hill, our fourth English actor on this list, is a longtime fan who brought his twenty-year-old copy of *The Lord of the Rings* to New Zealand with him. He wanted to be part of the project so much, he made his own audition tape, which he directed himself in a friend's barn.

6. **Bruce Hopkins:** *Nonfan.* Hopkins didn't know anything about the books when he got the part of Gamling.

7. **Miranda Otto:** *Nonfan.* When Otto was given the scripts, she read them in the wrong order, thinking *The Two Towers* was the concluding film, and was completely confused.

8. **Karl Urban:** *Fan.* The New Zealander read the books in the 1980s and reread them when he heard they were going to be filmed in his home country.

9. **Viggo Mortensen:** *Nonfan.* Mortensen had no idea who Aragorn was when he was offered the part, but his son was a big fan of the books and the Ranger.

10. **Sean Bean:** *Fan.* Bean read the books in his twenties and remembered them vividly when he first heard about the film project.

11. **Billy Boyd:** *Nonfan.* Boyd enjoyed *The Hobbit*, but he gave up on *The Lord of the Rings* when he saw it was about Frodo and not Bilbo.

12. **Dominic Monaghan:** *Fan.* Monaghan, whose father was a big fan, read the books as a teenager and loved them.

13. **Craig Parker:** *Fan.* Parker, a native of Fiji, was living in New Zealand when the project was announced. He had already read the books, and he began to reread them before landing the role of Haldir.

14. **Liv Tyler:** *Nonfan.* Tyler didn't know anything about the books and depended on her agent for advice.

15. **Orlando Bloom:** *Nonfan.* Bloom began reading the books at age fourteen, but he was distracted by other interests and did not finish them until becoming involved with the film project.

If your total score is:
1–4 correct: Frodo didn't fail, but you sure did.
5–8 correct: Fool of a Took!
9–11 correct: Gandalf would be proud.
12–15 correct: You have your own palantír, don't you?

Film or Book Invention?

1. **Book** — While Pippin is quite a bit younger when the long expected party takes place in the book, according to the appendices he's one of the guests.

2. **Book** — Tolkien's inscription description is perfectly matched in the films.

3. **Film** — In the books, the entrance to the tower faces east while the gate of Isengard is to the south.

4. **Film** — In Tolkien's version, while Frodo does spy the Nazgûl from the remains of the watchtower atop the hill, he is actually stabbed in a dell on the western flank of the hill.

5. **Book** — This really happened (if you accept the books as reality, like I do). Elrond and Círdan both asked Isildur, at Mount Doom, to destroy the Ring. Fortunately, for the sake of a good story, Isildur decided not to.

6. **Film** — Despite its importance, very little of Rivendell is actually described in the books. The Grand Chamber is not mentioned.

7. **Film** — Arwen does give Frodo a white gem in the book, but I don't think she had merchandising in mind there.

8. **Film** — The hair color of Legolas is never described in the book. There is one line where his head is described as dark, leading some to believe he has dark hair. Others argue that his head is dark only because its night-time, which still others dispute by pointing out that Tolkien describes it as a very bright night. I say his hair color should be whatever the reader wishes it to be.

9. **Film** — In the book, the Moon is waning as the company enters Moria and is "nearly spent" the first night after the company escapes.

10. **Film** — In the book, it's actually a frustrated Boromir who throws a stone in.

11. **Book** — In Bakshi's film they open inward, which actually makes it more difficult for the Watcher in the Water to close them. Jackson's film does it right.

12. **Book** — In the book, Gandalf tells Frodo this at Bag End. It's such a great line the scriptwriters had to work it in somewhere.

13. **Book** — The film changed a few gifts, but not this one.

14. **Film** — The scriptwriters invented them because they wanted to increase the believability that Gríma could have such control over the people of Rohan.

15. **Book** — This image, described in the book, was apparently too shocking for television viewers to witness. Weta was asked to superimpose an Orc helmet over it for TV broadcasts.

16. **Film** — There is an Éothain in the book, but he's one of the Riders of Rohan. In fact, most of the invented character names in the trilogy are either borrowed from somewhere in the books (such as Éothain), or not mentioned in the films (such as Lurtz). "Freda" is a rare case where the scriptwriters invented a name and used it right alongside Tolkien's creations.

17. **Book** — Described in Appendices A and B (and *The Silmarillion*), this very ancient heirloom was given to Aragorn when Elrond told him about

his lineage. In the book, Aragorn does not have it when he meets Frodo; he has already given it to Arwen.

18. **Book** — This is a trick question. You see, in the book the caves are not connected to the Keep, being some ways back in the valley. However, in the book the Keep is called "the Hornburg" while Helm's Deep is the entire valley.

19. **Book** — You'd think this was made up by a scriptwriter, but it's straight from the book.

20. **Film** — In Tolkien's story, while it's true that Denethor and Gondor know that the One Ring was made, it is believed, in the south, to have perished. When Denethor finds out he's mistaken, he laments that had Boromir lived, he would have brought him a mighty gift.

21. **Book** — While many filmgoers believed this to be an inside joke, it's one of the more touching parts of the books.

22. **Book** — It's not quite so dramatic in the book, but it's there. Gandalf says, "There they go speeding west," and mentions a few hills. Jackson and company show you what a score and majestic cinematography can do to turn a couple lines into a breathtaking scene. It's a moment I wish Tolkien could have seen on the big screen.

23. **Book** — It looks like a made-for-the-movies sort of thing; but Tolkien had a very visual imagination, and it was his idea.

24. **Film** — In the book, Denethor does ask Pippin if he can sing. However, Denethor never asks for a song.

25. **Book** — How could you miss him? He's mentioned . . . in one sentence.

26. **Book** — As a First World War veteran, Tolkien knew war as the terrible and brutal thing it is.

27. **Film** — In the book, Aragorn insists that the horses enter, because Tolkien was not as kind as the film with his geography. In the "real"

Middle-earth, the Anduin River is a long way from the exit of the Paths of the Dead, and Aragorn knows the horses are needed to reach it.

28. **Film** — Perhaps Tolkien would have enjoyed the beacons scene had he lived to see the films. However, as Denethor plunges to his death, I can't help but picture Tolkien rolling his eyes a bit as Jackson, somewhere else in the theater, nervously tries to avoid being seen by the old scribe.

29. **Book** — This day, March 15, is the focal point of the first half of Tolkien's *The Return of the King*, with five of its ten chapters touching upon it.

30. **Film** — In Tolkien's story, Théoden speaks to Merry and Éomer before he dies.

31. **Film** — In the book, Aragorn releases the Army of the Dead as soon as he gains control of the ships.

If your total score is:
1–10 correct: It's been a while since you've read the books, hasn't it?
11–20 correct: Apparently, Jackson isn't the only one with a muddled mind.
21–30 correct: Congratulations; Tolkien would be proud.
All 31 correct: You're Professor Tolkien, right?

Sources

Adams, Doug. "The Music of the Lord of the Rings Films." "The Annotated Score."

The Fellowship of the Ring, The Two Towers, and The Return of the King Complete Recordings. Reprise Records, 2005, 2006, 2007.

Astin, Sean with Joe Layden. *There and Back Again,* St. Martin's Press: New York, 2004.

Bakshi, Ralph. Email interview with author. August 22, 2002.

Bellas, Miles. Email interview with author. September 13, 2002.

Broadway, Cliff and Erica Challis, Cynthia L. McNew, Dave Smith, and Michael Urban. *The People's Guide to J.R.R. Tolkien,* Cold Spring Press: New York, 2004.

Broadway, Cliff. Email interview with author. October 22, 2002.

Carpenter, Humphrey. *The Letters of J.R.R. Tolkien,* Houghton Mifflin Company: Boston, 1981.

Carpenter, Humphrey. *J.R.R. Tolkien: A Biography,* Houghton Mifflin Company: Boston, 1977.

Cordova, Carlene. Email interview with author. May 20, 2008.

Davis, Warwick. Email interview with author. June 1, 2003.

Falconer, Daniel. Email interview with author. February 23, 2005.

Fisher, Jude. *The Lord of the Rings: The Fellowship of the Ring Visual Companion*, Houghton Mifflin Company: Boston, 2001.

—. *The Lord of the Rings: The Two Towers Visual Companion*, Houghton Mifflin Company: Boston, 2002.

—. *The Lord of the Rings: The Return of the King Visual Companion*, Houghton Mifflin Company: Boston, 2003.

Fonstad, Karen Wynn. *The Atlas of Middle-earth*, Houghton Mifflin Company: Boston, 1991.

Hartwell, Vance. Email interview with author. July 15, 2002.

Jackson, Peter, director *The Lord of the Rings: The Fellowship of the Ring*. DVD. New Line Cinema, 2001.

Jackson, Peter, director *The Lord of the Rings: The Two Towers*. DVD. New Line Cinema, 2002.

Jackson, Peter, director *The Lord of the Rings: The Return of the King*. DVD. New Line Cinema, 2003.

Kocher, Paul. *Master of Middle-earth*, Ballantine Books: New York, 1972.

Lasaine, Paul. Email interview with author. May 27, 2005.

Lordoftherings.net: online

Mckellen.com: online

Orc, Zac the. Email interview with author. October 25, 2003.

Russell, Gary. *The Art of The Fellowship of the Ring*, Houghton Mifflin Company: Boston 2002.

Russell, Gary. *The Art of The Two Towers*, Houghton Mifflin Company: Boston 2003.

—. *The Art of The Return of the King*, Houghton Mifflin Company: Boston 2004.

—. *The Art of The Lord of the Rings*, Houghton Mifflin Company: Boston 2004.

Serkis, Andy. *Gollum: A Behind the Scenes Guide of the Making of Gollum*, Houghton Mifflin Company: Boston 2003.

Shah, Kiran. Email interview with author. October 20, 2003.

Sibley, Brian. *Peter Jackson: A Film-Maker's Journey*, Harper Collins UK: London, 2006.

—. *The Lord of the Rings Official Movie Guide*, Houghton Mifflin Company: Boston, 2001.

—. *The Lord of the Rings: The Making of the Movie Trilogy*, Houghton Mifflin Company: Boston, 2002.

The Lord of the Rings Fan Club Official Movie Magazines. Vols. 1–18. February 2002–January 2005. Various articles.

TheOneRing.net: online.

Thompson, Kristin. *The Frodo Franchise*, University of California Press: London, 2007

Tolkien, J.R.R. *The Lord of the Rings*, Houghton Mifflin Company: Boston, 1991.

—. *The Hobbit*, Houghton Mifflin Company: Boston, 1988.

—. *The Silmarillion*, Houghton Mifflin Company, Boston, 1977.

Acknowledgments

It's tempting to pretend that the book you hold in your hands came about simply because of me. However, so many people had a hand in helping me make this book a reality, it's almost a shame that my name is the only one on the cover. (Almost!) While I can't name all of the hundreds of people who supported and aided me with this project, I would like to acknowledge some of them.

Thank you to Jack David and everyone at ECW Press for taking a chance on me and my idea. David Caron, Nikki Stafford, Emily Schultz, and Tania Craan were especially helpful in creating the illusion that I'm a competent, organized, and intelligent writer.

Thank you to my beta readers and fellow Tolkien fans Nick Lowery and Carina Gunder. Remember, if I messed something up, it's their fault. (I'm kidding!)

They say a picture's worth a thousand words, and so I'd like to give a thousand thanks to all who contributed photos, especially Thomas P. Wuellette and Ian Smith. I also must give just as big a thank-you to Jacquie Roland for her beautiful illustrations.

To all the fans, cast, and crewmembers of *The Lord of the Rings* who helped me with this project without any thought of a reward, proving once again that Ringers are the kindest people in the world, I can't tell you how grateful I am. I also can't tell Professor Tolkien how grateful I am for the work he did, because he's no longer around. However, I'd like to throw some thanks his way as well.

Thank *you*, the reader, for believing in me enough to give me this chance to entertain you. My greatest wish for this book is for you to feel it is worth the money you spent on it.

Finally, my biggest thanks to Keely, my own Lúthien, who helped me from the beginning and will always be the love of my life.

About the Author

J.W. Braun was a charter member of *The Lord of the Rings* Fan Club and has written articles for both **theonering.net** and **theonering.com**.

Growing up in the 1980s in the area where *Dungeons & Dragons* was invented, Braun developed an interest in fantasy at an early age and fell in love with *The Lord of the Rings* before he had even discovered girls.

Today he is married and enjoys sports, reading, playing the piano, and spending time with his family. He works at a bottle factory as a glass inspector.

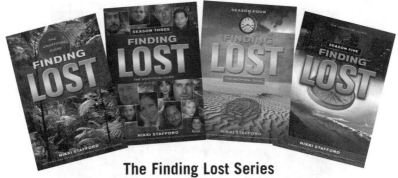

Also from ECW Press

The 100 Best Movies You've Never Seen
Son of The 100 Best Movies You've Never Seen
By Richard Crouse / $17.95 U.S./CDN

Movie buffs, discriminating renters and collectors, and fans of off-beat cinema: prepare to drool over film critic Richard Crouse's lists of the best overlooked and underappreciated films of the last 100 years. With his trademark insight and wit, Crouse covers a wide spectrum of films, from obscure masterpieces to little-seen classics that were groundbreaking for their time, but are now forgotten. Along the way he includes interviews with filmmakers and actors, memorable quotes, and quirky details. In *The 100 Best Movies You've Never Seen*, Crouse suggests movies such as *Bubba Ho-Tep*, *Cane Toads: An Unnatural History*, *Ginger Snaps*, *Hedwig & the Angry Inch*, and *The Terror of Tiny Town*, "the world's first (and to date, only) all-midget musical motion picture."

In his acclaimed followup, *Son of The 100 Best Movies You've Never Seen*, Crouse recommends such films as *The Junky's Christmas*, *Planet of the Vampires*, *Mayor of Sunset Strip*, and *The Cameraman's Revenge*, an obscure 1912 stop-motion animation film featuring mummified insects. With laugh-out-loud reviews, well researched insight, interviews with the cast and directors of the films, and *lots* of love for Roger Corman, Crouse will keep you entertained. If you want to read another take on that cult film you love and wish everyone else watched, or you just want a great recommendation for something to rent tonight, these are the books for you!